A HAUNTING EXISTENCE

KRISTY HINKLE AND MARIE CIPRIANO

Outskirts Press, Inc.
Denver, Colorado

The opinions expressed in this manuscript are solely the opinions of the author and do not represent the opinions or thoughts of the publisher.

A Haunting Existence
All Rights Reserved
Copyright © 2007 Kristy Hinkle and Marie Cipriano
V 3.0

This book may not be reproduced, transmitted, or stored in whole or in part by any means, including graphic, electronic, or mechanical without the express written consent of the publisher except in the case of brief quotations embodied in critical articles and reviews.

Outskirts Press
http://www.outskirtspress.com

ISBN-10: 1-4327-0567-9
ISBN-13: 978-1-4327-0567-1

Outskirts Press and the "OP" logo are trademarks belonging to Outskirts Press, Inc.

Printed in the United States of America

I want to thank those who made this book possible.

First and foremost Southern New England Paranormal, www.southernnewenglandparanormal.com, for their support.

Springfield Ghost Hunters Society, out of Springfield Ohio for inviting me along on investigations and allowing me to publish our findings.
www.springfieldghosthunter.com

Their Members;

Kathy Wolboldt,
Dave Frevert,
Dorothy Frevert,
John Middleton,
Niki Bailey.

Southern Ohio Paranormal, out of Cincinnati Ohio
www.southernohioparanomal.org

Their Members;

James Bell,
Brian Klein,
Brandon Acus,
Lorain (Rainie) Mendleson

Also, George J. Adams, and the management of Prospect Place Mansion, Dresden Ohio.
www.gwacenter.org/

Toni Hinkle
Kelly Heuser
Russ Heuser
Jessey Warner
Jonathan from Alabama.

To all our Family and Friends who supported us in our choices through out the years, this is for you!!
Thanks for everything!

I would also like to take this time to thank my inspiration. Aside from my family and friends, I would like to acknowledge Grant Wilson, Jason Hawes and the other members of TAPS.
www.The-Atlantic-Paranormal-Society.com

They are a great group of people and I am honored to know them

INTRO

This is an informative book, so that people who have had paranormal experiences know they are not alone. Join us in learning more about the phenomena that is sweeping the nation.

These are personal stories, from the writers, and people in our lives.

We chose to live our lives looking for answers to everyone's most nagging questions. Am I crazy to believe that I have had a paranormal experience? No, you are not and this book will show you that.

Southern New England Paranormal has been on a few very exciting investigations with other Paranormal investigation Groups, and some of those stories are reflected upon in here.

If you are interested in knowing the names of these groups and members please read the credits page for their names and email addresses.

These are true events; that we feel should be shared, to help others in need.

Written by:
Kristy Hinkle
&
Marie Cipriano

A HAUNTING EXISTENCE

This is the story of my family, who believe we are followed by such events no matter where we move to, or what we do to rid ourselves of these events.

This is a true story, and as accurate as I can remember things. Other stories, individual stories, from my five other siblings, my mother and father, may appear later on.

I was young when this all started, I remember that when I was about eight years old I had my first encounter with the unknown.

I shared a room with my sisters. The two of them were sound asleep at this hour. It had to be around three in the morning, at the least.

I could not sleep; I kept feeling as though someone was watching me. All night I felt this, and it was scaring me to think someone could be standing outside the window looking through. In my room, there were two sets of bunk beds, and I was laying in the far one, at the other side of the room.

I heard a rustling on the far side of the bedroom, when I opened my eyes, I saw a blue nightgown flowing. Thinking this was my mother, who often wore a blue nightgown, I tried to speak to her.

As I sat up, I saw that the woman in my room had grey hair, pulled into a bun. My mother has long brown, curly hair.

The woman turned and faced me, and lifted her finger to her mouth, as if she were saying shhh. I froze, as the woman appeared to be covering up one of my sisters with a blanket that she had kicked off.

I was an adventurous girl who was very curious as to whom this woman could be.

As the woman walked out of the room, I followed.

The woman led me down the hall, into the living room, and then rounded the corner into the kitchen, but by the time I got to the kitchen door, the woman was gone.

I turned on the television and watched late night programming, until my sisters woke up.

I told them all about the woman, and how she disappeared in the kitchen, but they did not seem to believe me.

I decided that I would not tell my mother, and just thought it had to have been a dream, after all no one can just vanish.

A few days later, one of them had a similar experience with the woman in the blue nightgown.

She told me, who no longer felt like I was a bit crazy and we both went to our mother together.

Our mother just told us, that if there was something in the house, it was not hurting anyone, and besides we were moving soon anyways, so it does not matter.

We could not move soon enough for us. Shortly after we came clean with our mother, a car hit our beloved cat, which was nearly thirteen years old, as he sat on the curb in front of our house. The cat was a white cat named Ghost; he was a free-range cat who came and went as he deemed fit. When he wanted in the house, he would knock on the front door, and meow. Our father buried the cat in the garden below our mother's bedroom window in the back. The next night, we heard a knocking at the door, but when we opened it, there was no one there.

It rained for about two days after that, during the last

night of rain, our mother heard some scratching on her bedroom window, but paid no attention to it. The next day as we played out side in the back yard, we noticed there was a big whole where we had buried the cat, up the side of the house there were paw prints, like that of a cat. We ran inside to tell our mother, but she already knew. There were muddy cat paw prints through her bedroom.

For the next few weeks, we kept hearing the knocking on the door, and the meowing of a cat that sounded like the raspy meow of our cat Ghost. Whose meow was unmistakable.

We finally relocated to a town far, from where we were living, we moved to a house that was around a hundred years old, and very big. It was red brick, with white trim, five bedrooms, and two bathrooms. There was an old bookshelf built into the wall, with what looked like an old toy box at the bottom of it. Casey, who was the second oldest of the six children, pulled up the lid one day, and found old newspapers. They were dated back to the Nineteen Fifties, when a brand new ironing board was only a few dollars.

We had not been in the house very long when we had to start school. We were not too happy about going to a new school, but knew we could not stay home all the time.

I was the first one to have something strange happen to me in this new house. I had been up late one weekend talking on the phone to some boy that I liked. I heard a noise coming from the kitchen, thinking it was one of my Siamese cats I went to go get the cat off the counter. I took the phone with me and was talking to this boy, but when I got into the kitchen there were no cats in sight and the cupboard doors were open. Thinking my father had been in there before leaving for work, I closed them and went back to the living room to talk with this guy some more.

I heard another noise, this one sounded like silverware hitting together, I cautiously walked back to the kitchen, phone in hand. I was not prepared for what I saw. The cupboard and cabinet doors were open again, but this time, so were the silverware and junk drawers. I closed them all, and told the boy on the phone what was going on. He laughed at me for being so gullible; he said it was probably my sisters messing with me. I went to their bedrooms, and found them sleeping. At this point, I started to worry, so I stayed in my room, talking on the phone, until about three in the morning when my father got home from work.

I ran down and told him what had happened and he just looked at me, and sent me to bed.

A few days later, Ryan my sister and Cory, our brother, together experienced a similar event, when they were up late watching movies.

It got to the point where things were disappearing in the house, keys, money, our parent's cigarettes and lighters. We would sit something down, and a few moments later when we went to get it, they would be gone.

After a few years of trying to ignore these things, I was now about sixteen years old I was talking with my boyfriend at the time about things that go on in that house. He had a great idea; he invited a few friends over to the house, and brought an Ouija Board.

I helped them get ready, by lighting candles, and having drinks ready for them if they needed them.

I had never played with an Ouija board, so I did not know what to expect.

I sat back and let him and his friends do what ever it was they were trying to do.

They asked to contact the spirit that is haunting the house, and a few more questions, suddenly the eye of the board started moving in a circle faster and faster. One girl went flying backwards and screamed. The candles were all blown out, and I ran for the light switch.

When I turned on the lights, the girl leading this whole thing, had this terrified look on her face, she was as white as a ghost herself. She hurriedly picked up her things, and ran out of the house. She apologized on her way out.

Her car sped off as the rest of them sat dumbfounded at the events. My boyfriend finally spoke, he told me that they had messed up, and things were not going to get better they would get worse.

I was unaware of exactly what they had done, and after all, I had not participated, so why would I be punished.

Shortly after that night, things had started getting worse, much worse. Items in the house would shoot across the room, and the silverware drawer would be emptied on the counter, as if someone had been looking for something.

One day, when I was hand washing the dishes, the entire front of the counter fell off and landed on my feet. Another time a cupboard door fell off its hinges and landed on top of my mothers head, giving her a nice big goose egg. Then one morning in the summer we all woke up to find our kitchen on fire. It was not a huge fire, but it could have been if we had not woken up when we did. The kitchen sustained minor smoke damage, and the cupboards were melted right above the stove. We put out the fire by throwing glasses of water on it.

Things did not subside in that house, and our family decided to move again. We had purchased a house down the road a few miles, but in the same school district.

The new house was quiet, no activity that we had noticed right away, we lived there comfortably for about six months. Then our dogs and cats started acting weird. The dogs would start barking and staring off at nothing in the corner of a room; the cats would not go into the basement anymore. I was the first one to notice this strange behavior, but did not think much of it, until I went in the basement to do laundry.

My cat, Shiva, followed me, and was acting strange. As I threw clothes into the washer, the cat was batting at my legs, and meowing. I looked up and saw a black mass standing in the corner, Shiva started to hiss, and I ran out of the laundry room as fast as I could. I told my siblings what I had seen and they were shocked, neither of them had seen anything, but knew something was going on. We all went down to the laundry room together to look for it, but we found nothing.

I did not sleep well for a while, but did not see anything and refused to do laundry alone.

One morning, we over heard our father talking to our mother. He had had a strange experience the night before as he slept. He said that he woke up because he could not breathe and saw a figure on a man sitting on his chest. He described the event in great length and detail. We were shocked, that the man, who used to have an explanation for everything that we had seen or heard, could not figure out what he had seen.

We lived in this house for just over a year, and then moved again.

It seemed that no matter where we lived, we would always experience something.

Even as adults, in our individual homes, we have things we cannot explain happening. We believe that we are doomed to have to deal with this for life.

Maybe there is something about my family, that we just cannot explain, but as of right now, we are all still haunted by things that take us all by surprise. From my Mom and Dad, all of my siblings and myself we are all plagued by these events regularly.

By:
Kristy Hinkle

THE 40 HOUSE

In July of Nineteen ninety-seven, three friends, and I decided to go look inside an old empty house down the street from where I lived. We had no idea at the time why or how long it had stood empty, but it had been for as long as we could remember.

We were walking down the street and closing in on the house. It had long been known as The Forty House, older residence around the small town in Ohio, called it The Demon House. The weeds were tall, and riddled with Poison Ivy and Ivy vines, wild flowers and shrubs.

Some of the Ivy vines were crawling up the side of the house, and in through broken widows. The Green paint was chipping away, and the old shudders were broken and falling off.

We worked our way through the over growth, the front of the house was inaccessible through the over growth, so we went up to the side of the house, where there was a screen door hanging from its hinges, the glass was broken and scattered everywhere.

We opened the unlocked door, knowing we were not the first to go exploring in this desolate location. Looking to the back of the house, we could see a rundown garage, and dusty shed.

An old broken cellar door, that appeared to have a busted lock hanging from it.

We walked into the side door, which led us into the kitchen; the light coming from the windows showed a lot of dust being kicked up into the air buy our movements. There were scattered plastic and broken glass dishes on the floor, busted cabinet doors, and ripped up papers all over the dirty yellow kitchen with the ugly green trim.

On a wall next to the door, was a wooden cabinet that contained a broken ironing board, and old heavy metal iron. Next to that was what appeared to be a hutch, with broken china, and old news papers in it. One of the newspapers had a date of September 17, Nineteen seventy-five on the top. We were mesmerized by this date, as we did not think this place was empty that long. Apparently, we were wrong.

We walked into the empty living room; we saw no personal items at all, just an ugly brown couch, and what was left of an old side table. There were damaged hardwood floors, and broken glass from the front door, and windows. In the middle of the floor was a dark stain, apparently from a leaky roof.

Slowly we made our way through the living room to the hall, and around to all the bedrooms. One that caught our attention appeared to have had a child's bed in it. The bed was only a frame and springs from an old mattress but, had a small doll sitting on top of it.

The room also had stains on the floor from another leak in the roof. We walked slowly through the house, and looked in closets, and rooms, and we attempted to go into the cellar. The cellar was creepy in itself. We did not even make it down a few steps when we heard what sounded like the cry of a dog. It startled us and we ran out of the house, only to laugh about this later.

One of our friends had neglected to tell us that when we were walking around the house, she had gone back for the doll that was in the bedroom. We saw it on our way back to the house. She said she was going to take it home, and give it to her niece.

A few weeks later, School had started back up and she pulled us aside at our lunch hour, to tell us a scary story about that doll she had taken home with her.

"I had put it in my mom's china hutch when we got home, you know the one in the living room, any how, a few days later, I went to get it out to take it to my niece and it was gone."

We all had a good laugh about this, in the beginning, but she just glared at all of us and continued to tell us that, a few days after that, when she was cleaning her room, she had found the doll under her bed.

"I thought it was my brother who had moved it, I yelled at him for trying to scare me and he looked at me like I was nuts and denied it.," she continued.

"I put it back in the cabinet and went on with my day, but later in the night I woke up to find it sitting on my night stand next to my bed. I threw it out of my room, and went back to sleep. It had been lying in the hall, but when I got up for school today, it was on my nightstand again. So I locked it in our shed before I got on the bus."

The look on her face was enough to tell us that she was not lying. She looked scared out of her mind.

"I want to take it back to the house." She said, "Will you guys come with me?"

We agreed, and arranged to go back to The 40 House after school that day.

We got off the bus at my house, to drop off our stuff, and then we walked to her house to get the doll from the shed.

When she unlocked the shed, with the key around her neck, it was gone. The doll that she claimed had been right there on a shelf was no longer in the shed.

"And you are sure your brother didn't take it?" Asked one of us.

"He couldn't have, he was in bed when I put her in

there." She claimed.

"Well, it's gone now. So I guess there is nothing we can do about it." I said. "If it comes back, hold on to it, and come get us!"

The weeks past quickly and the days were still hot. It was mid-August when our friend and her brother showed up at my house on a Saturday night, wanting to go back to The 40 House. It was about nine o'clock at night, and I was working on a History report for school, in our office. My mother was highly against me going and told me if she ever caught me at that house, she would ground me for a month. Being 17 at the time, I was not trying to be grounded. Therefore, I sent my older sister with them to the house. She was over twenty-one so my parents could not stop her.

As I sat in the office with the window that looked over the front porch open, waiting for their return I was writing my History paper. I heard something that I will never forget. A dark and mean sounding voice screaming in my head, "Get them out! Get them OUT!" In my minds eye, I saw something glowing red, like eyes or something of that nature.

Thinking it was my imagination-running wild I laughed and went back to my work.

Suddenly there was screaming and yelling coming from the road, and I saw my sister, Kelly, with our friends running back towards the house.

I starred at them in wonder, thinking they were just crazy people scared of the dark, when they came to the window, I noticed they were obviously scared and out of breath.

Kelly started rambling and stumbling over her words, one of the friends Jumped in and started talking fast.

"Something in that house." (He coughs) "There is something in there. I swear it."

His sister, who had appeared a bit calmer about it broke in and started explaining.

"We went in there, and walked around. Nothing out of the ordinary, except that it was dark. We went to the back bedroom, and the doll was in there. Back on the bed where I had found her."

For a minute, I did not believe it. I rather thought that they had faked it. Then Kelly, finally able to talk said.

"There were these Bright Red eyes, watching us. In the living room."

"That could have been tail lights on a car Kelly, its right next to the road." I told her.

Vigorously they all three shook their heads no. "It wasn't tail lights. They moved towards us. He was attacked, by something. His flash light went flying across the room." Kelly explained.

"Yeah, Dads going to kill me. That was his best flash light." He mumbled.

"It kept saying something in a horrible voice." Kelly continued.

I stopped for a minute. "Get Out." I whispered.

"Yeah… " Kelly said. "How did you know?"

"I heard it." I said. "Well, sort of. I heard. 'Get Them OUT!' and I thought it was my imagination running wild again, and I saw something glowing red in my mind."

"Really?" My friend asked.

"Yeah." I told her, lowering my head. "So, where's the flash light?"

"Still there. I wasn't going back for it." He Said.

"So were you hurt? They said you got attacked, were you hurt?" I asked

"Sort of, it doesn't really hurt, just stings a little." He Said lifting his shirt.

Across his back were four scratches from one side to the other. They looked like welts, with a few drops of blood poking through the skin.

"Wow, that's creepy." I said.

A few days later, In the light of day, we went to look

for their dad's flash light. He wanted to give it back to his dad.

We found it in the front yard of the house, so we did not even need to go inside.

"It wasn't here." He said.

"Huh?" I asked.

"It wasn't here. It was inside, in the living room."

"Oh well, It's out here now, and we don't have to go inside." I smiled.

As we started back towards the street, we heard a scream, it sounded like a woman's voice. We looked back at the house, and headed, quickly, to my house.

Later, upon talking to a shopkeeper at the local corner market, I found out that, in 1975 sometime, a family of four was murdered in that house. A woman, a man and their two children. The person who killed them was never caught.

I recently went back to the location, now ten years later, and the house is no longer standing. They sold the land and now on the location where The 40 House once stood, there is a housing development.

I hope they remembered to bless the land before building anything there, but knowing these homebuilders now a days, they did not.

Some names have been omitted to protect the not so innocent.

By:
Kristy Hinkle

A VISIT FROM A FRIEND

On September 14th 1996, a close friend passed away in a car accident. He was two weeks away from his eighteenth birthday.

They say he was speeding down a back road in Pataskala Ohio, when he hit a pot hole, and lost control of the his car, over corrected and hit a tree. The 1995 Ford Escort he was driving split in half, the seatbelt had broken, no air bags deployed and he was thrown from the car. After his death, we painted a cross, with his name, date of birth and date of death on it, and we stuck it in the ground at the spot where he had died.

We attended his showing in Pataskala, where I attempted to read a poem that I had written; I was unable to speak through my tears, so my older sister had to read it.

A few days later, we drove down to Kentucky for his funeral; he was buried where the rest of his family had been.

A very short time followed that, when we started seeing Jared around. It only happened for a short time, but it made a strong impact on all of our lives.

Jared was the boyfriend of my younger sister at the time of his death, he and I had our differences, and I never forgot the day he had passed. He and I had an argument about him being afraid of getting wet in the rain; I called him a City Boy. We were both angry at that time, and I never did get to apologize for the argument.

A little, while after the funeral we all noticed things, one at a time. Sometimes it would be something small, like keys disappearing, jewelry moving from one place to another.

One day I went down to do laundry my ponytail was flipped up when I was standing still, that was a clue as to what was going on. Jared used to hit my ponytail if he was standing behind me.

One night when my dad came home from work, he claims to have seen him sitting in a chair in the kitchen. Without thinking, he told him, "Get out of my seat." Then he realized that it was not possible for him to be sitting there, he turned and Jared was gone.

In our house, there was some sort of on going battle over one particular chair at the breakfast bar in the kitchen. It was a red high back chair, that I did not find too comfortable, but Jared used to fight over that chair with my sister Kelly and our dad.

Jared's mother told us about her cat running around the house, and hissing at Jared's bedroom door, as though he were in there. The cat did not like Jared, at all.

My sister says she saw him walking through our hallway once. Our dogs, which Jared absolutely adored, would stomp around the living room, as if they were playing with an unseen person. The male husky would go in to a 'pounce' stance and bounce up and down, exactly the way he did when Jared came over and would play with him. Our cats would freak out, and fall off the counters as if someone who was not there had startled them. As Jared had a tendency to do when he was over visiting.

We all had our encounters with Jared's spirit. Coming by to tell us he was still around, that he still remembered all of us, even from the other side.

By:
Kristy Hinkle

This Story is short, because the disturbances only lasted for a few short weeks. Jared is now at rest, and we have not seen him or heard from him in a long while.
Nevertheless, we still remember him and love him.

In Memory of Jared D. Lowery
Died September 14th 1996
Your memory is with us, always!

CHIEF

In May of Nineteen ninety-seven, my family moved to a new home, I was eighteen years old, and finally able to come in late. It did not take long for things to get crazy around this house.

The week after we moved in, my mom had been out side with her dogs admiring the view of the stars and a big open field of nothing that stretched as far as the eye could see, behind the new house.

She came in the house, looking pale and shaken up, she headed straight for her bedroom, but we stopped her.

"Mom, what's wrong?" My sister asked.

"You wouldn't believe me if I told you." She said.

"Ha Ha, Try me. " I said with a laugh.

"I think I just saw a UFO." She claimed.

"Ok your right. I don't believe that." I said giggling.

"No, really, I was standing on the porch, and I saw a white light. It lit up the whole sky." She explained.

"We didn't see anything." I said.

"Oh." She said. "I am going to bed."

A few days later, I had gone out with some friends and came home late. My sister Kelly was with me in the living room as I watched television. She got up and went to the bathroom.

I saw something move out of the corner of my eye, I was about to ask Kelly to get me a pop when I noticed it was on the other side of a half wall we had in there, but there was a computer desk right on the other side of that wall. Through the small pillars, I could see a form, a black mass looking form. It began to move. It came to the opening between the half walls, and stopped, he looked at me.

As I sat there in awe of what I was seeing, I noticed he looked like a Native American. He had long braids down his shoulders and an old, wise looking face.

I starred at him, as he turned and walked down the hall. I heard the bathroom door open and close, and I yelled.

"Kelly?" I asked.

"Yeah?" she answered.

"Were you just in here?"

"No, I went to the bathroom."

"Oh. Ok…" I stumbled

"Why?"

I explained to her what I had seen, and then went to the kitchen for a glass of water and a bowl of macaroni salad. She followed me in there, not wanting to be alone, I guess.

"What do you think it was?" She asked.

"If I knew that, I wouldn't be asking where you were." I told her.

After morning came, I told everyone in the house, what I had seen. My family thought I was nuts, my dad did not believe in anything like this, and was the type of person who says. 'You don't get enough sleep and you are seeing things.' but I stuck to my story.

Over the next few weeks, everyone was starting to see and hear things around the house, except dad who slept during the day and worked all night.

One morning when I got up, my mom was sitting on the back deck, drinking her coffee; I grabbed me a cup and sat down with her. We sat there, drinking our coffee and

smoking cigarettes.
"You weren't lying." She said.
"Huh? About what?"
"The man you saw, I saw him last night. I woke up because I thought your dad came home, and sat down on the bed without turning on the television, and when I asked him what he was doing home so early, he did not answer me, I sat up and there was a man sitting on the foot of my bed and it was not your dad. I went to turn the light on, but he disappeared." She explained.
"Oh. Creepy." I said.
After a few weeks, the stories from siblings and my parents started sweeping through the house. Everything from, the laundry detergent falling off a high shelf, without being touched to doors opening and closing.
We dubbed this presence Chief, It suited him. He was a playful spirit, not harming anyone in anyway. I think he liked having us around.
In the middle of 1999, I moved in with my boyfriend, Jessey, right next door to this house, The two houses were pretty close together, and there were several times when I would pass between the house going out to a bon fire. I would see Chief standing in the bay window at the side of that house, he looked sad when I saw him. I would always wave to him, and smile. It is not as if I was totally gone, I was right next door, and frequently went over there.
Until my parents moved out over the holidays in 1999.
At the stroke of Mid-night, on New Years, the year 2000, we all heard a horrible bang sound coming from the house next door. We still had the keys so we went over there to see what was going on and we found that the water heater had exploded in a wall of water down the hall of this house. All of the water pipes were bursting. It was wintertime, but it was not that cold outside. The whole kitchen was flooding. The pipes in the kitchen sink exploded, along with the pipes under the hall way and

bathroom, and even under the dining room. There was no explanation for this, as most of the pipes were new. It was not cold enough to freeze them, and the heat was still on in that house. .

Shortly after that, I met a man who worked at the gas station that I frequented. His name was Mike. He told me about his wife who was a Cherokee; she had a lifetime of knowledge of the Native American way of life. I had decided one day to go and meet her.

We became fast friends. She lived right across the street from my parent's old house. We talked a lot about the things that had gone on in there, and in the place where I lived.

A few years later, after my parents moved out of town, and I still lived in that house next door, new neighbors bought the house. I was half-tempted to tell them about Chief, but they were very hateful people. I was sitting with Nikki one day, when she told me that her and her son Brian had been sitting out side facing my parent's old house, when they saw a great big ball of white light, raise from the house and explode in the sky, lighting up the night sky, as though it was mid-day. I told her that years ago, my mom had said the same thing, and it had been only a week since the new neighbors had moved in to that house. Same time period that we had lived there when my mom saw it.

Nikki told me that it was a curse, A Native American curse that will never go away, no matter who lives in that house. It will affect everyone who lives there. Upon doing some research on that house, I had found out that before we lived there, four other families in the last few years went bankrupt and lost the house to foreclosure. However, the difference with my family is none of the pipes had torn out the floors when the other families moved out.

Nikki said this was grief being shown by Chief, as he grew to like us and did not want us to leave. I later found out that the elders in the area believe that a major battle had taken place here between Native American Tribes. Many were killed, and buried here. Not too hard to believe, considering there were Indian Mounds scattered around the area.

The way I was told, the people who owned the house when I lived out there, are no longer staying at this house. I am not sure what happened, but apparently, Chief did not like them as much as he did us.

Kristy Hinkle

THE ATTACK

This event took place in year Two Thousand, shortly after the birth of my first child. This in fact happened to me, and involves my child.

I lived in a house that I had never really been comfortable in; it just had a feeling to it that gave me goose bumps.

I was sleeping soundly one night, after putting the baby down. He was only a few weeks old. I woke up in the middle of the night, to him crying, I picked him up out of his crib, walked to my bed, the television was on, and I was watching some late night show, Rocking Anthony back to sleep. I noticed that my lap all of the sudden was really light, and I had a cool breeze where he had been laying. I looked down and the baby was gone. I freaked out and jumped to my feet, rushed over to his bed and looked for him.

He was sound asleep in his crib. Thinking, to my self, I really needed some sleep, that I had dreamed the whole thing. Wow, I was tired if I could dream that I had taken him out of his crib, fed him and tried rocking him back to sleep. Just to find my self-sitting up in my bed watching television.

I needed coffee! It was only three in the morning, but I

had had enough sleep for one night.

As I headed towards the bedroom door, I felt a hand on my shoulder. I stopped, and looked back; hand on the doorknob, thinking it was Jessey.

Standing there behind me was a ghostly figure, she was white, and I could see right through her. She looked half-decayed, and had her long tangled hair in her face.

I was in such shock at the sight of her that I could not scream, I opened my mouth and nothing came out.

She lunged at me, grabbing me by my neck, and she hurled me at the door.

I hit the door, and fell into the wall, knocking into the baby's crib. He woke up, and started to cry. Jessey heard the commotion and woke up. He ran over to me.

"What happened?" He asked.

I still could not speak, he picked up Anthony, and we all went to the kitchen.

We sat down at the kitchen table and he turned on the light.

He handed the baby to me, and I noticed that he had scratches on his face, just three small welt like scratches down his cheek. He could not have done this himself as he was wearing a sleeper with paw like mittens on it. I showed it to Jessey and then handed the baby back to him. I went to the bathroom, where I looked in the mirror, thinking I was going out of my mind.

I had red marks on the front of my neck, and eight little punctures on the back. I immediately went back to the kitchen and showed Jessey. Our roommate Andy, who had just arrived home from work, came out of his room down the hall to see what was going on. We showed him the marks, and I explained to both of them what had happened.

They both tried to convince me that I had been sleep walking, but I know what I saw.

I stayed up for the rest of the night, holding my pentacle in my hand tightly, as I watched the sun come up. After eight in the morning, I ran next-door, to my parent's house, and told my sisters and my mom what had taken place.

"Do you know who it was?" Shannon asked.

"Not a clue." I told her.

For the next few nights, I stayed in the living room, with Anthony in a small bassinet next to the couch. Finally, I spoke with a friend of mine from a spiritual store. She told me to ask around and find any and all information on that house that I possibly can. Then she gave me a way to cleanse the room, and the house.

I had nowhere to look except with Jessey's parents who had lived in that house for twenty-five years or so. When I sat his father down, and asked him about the disturbance. He informed me that there were several unexplained things that had happened there, and he was afraid to tell anyone about them. He proceeded to tell me that when he lived there, being the night owl that he was, he would often times see a glowing gold figure walk down the hall and disappear into the last bedroom on the left. That was now Andy's room. He also told me of an encounter with what he thought was an angel, but ended up saying some horrible things to him, and he chased it away using the lords name.

"I can't tell you how many times, I heard my name called, or the kids wouldn't sleep in their own rooms, they were scared of something." He explained.

"Are you sure they were scared of something? Jessey says he has never seen anything in this house, and he's been here his whole life." I said

"Oh yeah, I'm positive, He was worse when he was younger, and he wouldn't remember this anyways. He grew out of it by the age of seven." He explained. "But we saw lots of things, and heard lots of things. In addition, Spunky, his dog would stand in the middle of the living room and start barking, and there was nothing there. Several people who have partied here, and slept over have claimed to hear or see something."

"Have you ever had the house blessed?" I asked
"No." He said.

I was not too sure that this cleansing spell would work. We would just have to wait and find out.

I went around the house, with Sea Salt and a Sage smudge stick, and conducted the ritual that had been given to me by the woman at the spiritual store. I buried protection stones in the yard at the four corners of the house, and chanted the spell given to me.

(Photograph by, Kristy Hinkle)

Later that night, I was ready to see how I did. We all went to bed, and slept wonderfully, the house felt more comfortable.

Though it did not rid us of all the wondering spirits, it did get rid of the negative entity.

We still sat in the living room some nights and watched the residual haunting, of the man in white, make his way down the hall and into the back bedroom. At the same time, every single night, he would do this. After a while, though it lost its thrill, and we just ignored it.

I lived in that house, for another 4 years without any more negative entities ruining my nights. I gave birth to a second child in January of 2002, and never once found a mark on him, that he did not put there himself.

Other events that happened in that house were not scary, more like intriguing to me.

I was never injured again, and I was still entertained by the residual haunting of the man in white walking down the hall every night, my oldest child had a visit from who we believe was his great grandmother on his father's side. We were sitting in our bedroom with Anthony on his fathers lap, he was about nine months old, and his younger brother had not been born yet. Anthony not yet really speaking looked up at the ceiling and started waving, he said, 'bye bye Dory, bye, bye.' We were not sure at the time what this was about, Jessey had never met his grandparents, and they passed before he was born. We asked around in the family and Jessey's mother informed us that his grandmother's name was Dory. This made more sense to us, it was Jessey's first child, and I believe that his grandmother was checking in on the family.

Kristy Hinkle

THE NIGHT JOB

I have worked several places since I was sixteen years old. I started out like many others at a local fast food restaurant I never imagined I would encounter things like this in the future.

Now, being a stay at home mom, I remember these events as clearly, as if they happened yesterday.

First, I worked at an old Bar. It was not the best place for a new mom to be working, but it was some cash in my pocket. I started out on the night shift and quickly gained the trust of the management for my strong work ethic and speed. I was moving up the ranks from a simple server to a full bartender.

A bit of history on this place is in order I believe. I started working there in February of two thousand two, not too long before I started there, in January a young man was caught in the cross fire of a bar fight that ended up in bullets flying in the parking lot. He was an innocent by stander, only trying to make his way to his car after closing. He died there in the parking lot.

Many nights that I was working the late shift, we would clean up, sweep, and get everything set up for the next morning, pushing in all the chairs, covering all the alcohol, washing all the dishes, and so on.

I remember one night, sitting in the manager's office doing final counts and staring at the monitors out of boredom, and nothing better to do. I saw a shadow walk across the floor. I jumped up thinking that someone was in the club after closing as we were all sitting in the office, I went to check, and there was no one out there. When I came back, my manager asked me why I ran out. I told him honestly I thought I saw someone. He told me not to worry about it that is what we have bouncers for, that it is not my job to handle people.

I brushed it off, and went home for the night. The next night I came in and got to listen to the day manager yell and scream at all the closers for the mess that we left the bar in before we left. I went around and double-checked everything, and the place was spotless. He claimed that chairs were everywhere, trashcans were tipped over, and the stage lights were left on.

This came as a shock to me. It was not like that when I left, and I left the same time as everyone else.

A few nights later, I showed up for my shift and was told a similar story by the day bartender. This did not ring true, and my night manager told them that we have been doing our jobs. That he was there, he knew what the place looked like when we left.

I was moved to the day shift for a while to cover for someone who had just had a baby, and when I came in, I noticed the bar was a mess, as described by many other people. I knew my night servers were in fact doing their jobs, but I could not imagine why the place would look like that.

The day manager called me in at seven in the morning, when my shift did not start until eleven. He called me in a panic, and said I had to get to the club, that he was too far away to get there, and someone had broken in. He wanted me to handle the police. I called the night manager, after all it was not my job to go in there and deal with the police in that situation.

I went anyways and showed up at the same time as the night manager, whom I might mention had a key to the place, that I did not have.

When we arrived there, we were informed by the police that the security alarm had gone off, and they needed us to let them in to the building because the disturbance was inside, and there was no sign of forced entry. The alarm company called and told us it was the motion alarms that were going off.

He opened the door for them and disabled the silent alarm. They made us stay in the lobby area, while they looked inside. When they came out they informed us that there was no one inside to account for the disturbance. He and I went into the bar and looked around; we were not prepared for what we saw. The bar was completely trashed, chairs were all over the place, tables were turned over, brooms and trashcans lying on the floor, and alcohol bottles tipped over.

After the initial shock wore off, we finally were able to speak to each other, but it was only briefly. I asked him if he had done a run through last night before leaving and he swore to me that he had. I called in my sister, who was also a server at the bar, to come in early and help clean up.

There were many times when we came in and found the bar that way, and even more when we were pulled out of bed by the police, and the alarm company saying the motion alarms were tripped.

When I went back to night shift, I was determined to find out the root cause of all the disturbances. I walked around the place many times before closing, marking down detailed accounts for where everything was, and what all had been done during clean up. The day shift would write down the state of things when arriving in the morning. This became a new rule when closing and opening. Even when I was not one of the people closing, I would make sure to check all the records on a daily or semi-daily basis.

I noticed several discrepancies, in the records. Such as, chairs marked as pushed in on the night shift, were strewn about on the day shift, and things such as trash cans being turned over, and the DJ booth being locked from the inside, when that was not possible.

At nights, I paid close attention to the monitors, and watched for anything strange. One night when we had an after party for a high rolling client, I was watching monitors as I had nothing else to do, and I saw the figure again. I watched it closely as it moved around the club, and then it was gone. I kept watching the video feed, and as I watched closely with my sister and another server close by we all saw it. The chairs started moving out from under tables, bar stools moved as well. We were all amazed and we ran to the private room and grabbed the manager's wife who was on duty as assistant manager. By the time we got back to the office, they had stopped. We explained to her what we had seen and she laughed at us.

She did not start to believe us until a few weeks later when I showed her some of the documents from clean up and opening, then she started getting a bit confused, knowing I would not fabricate the clean up log, she decided one night to watch for herself.

The next night after staying there most of the night before, she approached me and told me she believed me. She had seen similar things the night before, she looked pale as a ghost, and could not believe she was actually talking about this with me.

Soon after we hired a new server named Sam, she was a sensitive person who knew immediately something was not right about that place. She did not work there very long, only a few weeks. Something scared her so bad during clean up that she left mid shift and never came back. No warning or reason she was gone. She left her tray on the bar and her street clothes in the locker room.

She had been cleaning the area behind the stage, and just ran out. We never heard from her again.

I do not know what happened to her, and I wish she would have waited and told someone and we could have worked with her.

After that, no one wanted to clean up behind the stage, afraid of what they would see or hear. I made them do it in pairs; two or three at a time would usually go back there. When it was my turn, I did not take any help with me, and was reprimanded for it shortly there after.

The assistant manager wanted to make sure we always took someone with us when we went to go back there. She was just as scared as most of the others.

There was one day that we were just having fun and enjoying the night shift when I looked up and saw some one sitting on the side of the stage. It was after closing, and we were cleaning up. I went to tell him that we were closed and he needed to leave, but when I got to the other side, he was gone. There was nowhere for him to go, there were no doors, and no way he could have gotten away with out me seeing him.

I transferred to the day shift permanently after that, and did not have any more encounters.

I asked around to see if people who worked there with me would be interested in sharing their stories, and none of them will talk about it.

Kristy Hinkle

THE NEW HOUSE

I purchased a new house in February of 2005; I am a very sensitive person so my first instincts were that the house was clear of all entities. I did not know how wrong I was.

It happened almost immediately after we moved in to the house, my boyfriend had gone exploring to see if he could find any remaining items in the attic, and see if there was room for storage up there. The attic had been at one time a wooden door on the ceiling, with a pull down ladder, but was now covered over with a piece of drywall. He broke into the attic, and that is when it all started.

I believe that something was at rest in there, and the previous owners knew it, and that is why it was boarded up.

A short while later my children started talking about seeing a little girl named Heidi, jumping on the roof of the house across the street. It was not long after that, that Heidi was at our house, playing in their playroom. My youngest Mathew has been caught several times talking to no one. When asked about this, he claims to have been talking to himself, even when he had mentioned Heidi's name loudly and we heard it. He would never talk about Heidi, when asked about her, he makes up a story. I do not know why he does not think he can tell us about her. His older brother Anthony called her The Bad Heidi, but Mathew describes her as his imaginary friend.

A little time passed, and I started hearing noises in the play room, being as it is attached to their bed room, I automatically assumed it was them playing when they should be in bed.

I would hear small voices, toys moving around and the battery-operated toys will turn on and off. They would fall off of things, and slam on the floor. We started taking notice when they started coming in our bedroom as well.

I woke up one night out of a deep sleep, to see a woman standing at the foot of my bed. She was very slim, with what I could tell was long hair. She was just a black form, but you could tell it was a woman. I asked her what she wanted and got no answer at first. After the second time she finally said, 'I need to tell you.' In a voice that sounded a lot like my best friends voice, but that was all she said. I asked what she needed to tell me and she just said 'I need to tell you, its important.' and then she was gone. I was confused and I just rolled over and went back to bed. A few nights later, I saw her again; only this time she was standing right next to my bed. I asked her again what she wanted and she did not answer, just disappeared. The following day, during an afternoon nap, I awoke with a strange feeling of being watched. Staring me right in the face was a very skinny woman, pale face, strong features, and long black hair. She was lying right beside me in my bed. Before I could ask her anything, she vanished. This was broad daylight. I did not think that in broad daylight I could see something like this.

That was the last time I saw the slim woman, but not the last time my nights would be interrupted. Many more nights proved restless, I was repeatedly awakened by figures standing by my bed, or in the middle of the room. They would make noises, and bump into the bed. Some nights I would not see them at all, they would just shake the bed to make their presence known.

That is when the footsteps started; they would stomp up the stairs, and open the back door.

There were many mornings I would wake up to find my back door standing wide open after it had been locked. We would come home from the ice cream shop or a family visit, and our dog would be out in the back yard, when we knew we had not left him out.

Some nights it sounded as though someone were trying to break into the house, or was already in the house, and going through our things down stairs. I would wake up my boyfriend and make him go and investigate, thinking someone was in the house. He got sick of not finding anyone, so he started calling the noises my boogiemen. Every time I would hear a noise it was always, my boogey men, and he would tell me to look for my self or ignore it.

I had to learn how to ignore it, but it was not easy. After I started ignoring it, things got worse and more pronounced. The children were terrified to go to either the upstairs or downstairs alone.

I started keeping an internet blog on my My Space for my friends to read, it was mostly about all the things going on in this house. Here are a few of the entries:

Friday, April 14, 2006

My boogey men/women

Wow, you aren't going to believe this. I have told you all in the past about my "visitors" in my home. Well they are getting out of control. Yesterday I took my boys out to lunch and to the arcade, when we got home my dog Storm was outside. I never leave him out side! He is a pure bread Husky, and I don't trust people! I made the boys stay in the car with Jessey while I checked to see if anyone was in the house and there was no one! My back door was wide open, but the screen door was closed.

5:37 PM - **0 Comments** - **0 Kudos** - **Add Comment** - **Edit** - **Remove**

Tuesday, April 18, 2006

ahhhhh
Current mood: exhausted
Category: Dreams and the Supernatural

I have written in my blogs about my spirit visitors before, and I just wanted to update all of you on them. Apparently they have decided to no longer bothering me in my bed. Which makes me happy, but last night I heard voices. Children's voices! My kids were in bed, I went in to check on them, and it sounded like 2 or 3 children were playing in the boys' play room. But they were asleep and there was no one in their play room. The noise continued through the night. I must have checked on the boys half a dozen times. (They aren't very good at faking asleep - so I know they really were sleeping) the last time I checked in on them was about 3 am. finally I figured it wasn't going stop, how Anthony and Mathew slept through it I don't know, so I turned my bed room box fan on high and opened my bedroom window (street noise) to drown out the playful giggles. Unfortunately I was up all night. I finally fell asleep around the time Jessey was getting up for work, at 6 am and by then the boys were awake. Watching TV in my room. So I'd say all and all I slept for maybe an hour. Jessey left at 7 am for work and I had to wake up to watch the kids. I love having these gifts to see and hear things. But sometimes it is a pain in the rump... Lots of sleepless nights because they won't let me sleep. They always choose to come out after I go to bed. Even after I tell them not to bother me at bed time. I guess at least they are enjoying themselves in boys' play room and not in our bed rooms I can't really complain. They have only woke Anthony up once and that was a couple days ago. I think my children and Jessey are just more sound sleepers than me. It's that mommy thing still. You moms and some of you dads know what I am talking about, when you are such

a light sleeper that you wake up if your child coughs in his/her sleep from across the hall. I have very good ears too, which makes it that much worse! When one of them knocks toys off of their beds that they insist on sleeping with. I can hear it. Oh well, I guess this is another one of those things I need to learn to deal with. My abilities are getting sharper with every meditation session, and I have to get used to hearing them at all hours. (Maybe I should get a night light?) I do however hate feeling like a child when there are monsters under the bed, or in the closet. I am not really afraid of these things. I am just not used to them popping up at all hours of the night, and some of them give off such negative vibes. Giving me a horrible feeling. I don't like that. But you have to take the bad with the good.
11:11 AM - **0 Comments** - **0 Kudos** - **Add Comment** - **Edit** - **Remove**

Tuesday, May 09, 2006

A person
Category: <u>Dreams and the Supernatural</u>
When I went to get a movie for the boys the other night, I went to the living room to get one off the shelf, I saw Jessey walk up stairs, and a few seconds later I heard footsteps, and glanced back and thought I saw Jessey walking towards the kitchen. I noticed he hadn't turned on the kitchen light, so I went to see what he was doing, and he wasn't in there. Thinking he was trying to sneak up on me again, I walked through the kitchen in to the dining room, and turned on the light and he wasn't there either. I went up stairs and he was in our room. I asked him if he had come back down stairs and he said no. Oh well, I wish I would've gotten a better look at this guy. First Shadow People and now full bodied apparitions. I need to set up some sort of film equipment! I just need to get some.
3:05 PM - 0 Comments - 0 Kudos - Add Comment - Edit - Remove

July 4th
Current mood: exhausted
Category: Dreams and the Supernatural

Well, Last night we took the kids to the fireworks. We ended up sitting in the car the whole time to watch, because naturally, it rained all night. When we got home, we all went to bed. For the first time in a week, I fell straight to sleep. Only to be woke up 2hrs later by my dog barking... Stormy doesn't bark. Not at night, anyways. So I was a bit startled. I didn't think much of it, until I tried to fall back asleep. I started hearing noises again. It sounded like someone shuffling through some of my papers on my downstairs hall bookshelf. (It's a very short book self) I decided to get up and turn on the TV. It was 1am. According to my Direct TV clock. I went to the bathroom and made sure that I walked heavily... I climbed back into bed, and closed my eyes, and heard some thumping. I listened for a minute, and realized that my cat had waited until late at night to play with his jingling ball in the next room. Calmed by this I tried again to sleep. And I left the TV on. lol (I seem to do that a lot lately) I heard some foot steps coming from my kitchen, and my dog started barking again. I heard the back door open and close. At this point I thought maybe someone was in my house. I Got up and turned on the downstairs light, and went down. There was no one there, the door was closed, and the dog was very unsettled and walking in circles. I finally fell asleep at around 2:30am. I am starting to get tired of this. I am losing a lot of sleep over this! It appears to be getting worse, after a long stint of silence around here!

12:19 PM - **4 Comments** - **0 Kudos** - **Add Comment** - **Edit** - **Remove**

These are just a few of the many Blog entries I have on My Space. I did not realize how many there actually were until I went back through them. These are some examples of what I have been dealing with. Maybe someday soon we will be able to find real proof of the visitors in this house.

One day when my children were playing in their room, I walked by their door, and they yelled for me. I stopped and they proceeded to tell me that their sisters were saying bad words. They do not have any sisters, so I asked them what their sisters names were, and they answered Linda, and Heidi. My oldest said there was a boy too, but the name is so strange, he had to have made it up, Bejumikka or something similar to that. I am guessing those are the names of the children, that I hear playing in there every night.

After a short period of silence around my house, I actually started sleeping better, getting around seven hours compared to the one to four hours I had been getting.

I had a rough night, and could not get to sleep; I do not know why I was just uncomfortable.

I went to the bathroom; the hall light was on for the children, who were afraid of the dark.

As I left my bedroom I heard something on the stairs, I turned to find a black shadow figure standing there. It appeared to be male; when I blinked my eyes, he was gone.

I went to the bathroom, as I went back to my room, I just felt a chill, as if someone was watching me. As I lay in bed trying to sleep, I heard what sounded like someone walking with heavy feet up my stairs, sort of, like when Jessey would get home from work and wear his steal toed work boots up the stairs; I could actually hear what sounded like his untied shoestrings tapping on the steps as he walked. My bedroom door was standing open, to listen for the children, but I still heard it creak as if it were opening.

I turned the TV on and waited to see what came in the door, but nothing was there. I did not sleep for the rest of the night.

This keeps re-playing in my life, there are nights when I cannot get to sleep at all, then there are nights, when I sleep like a baby.

Jessey has heard things around this house too, but he will not admit too much of it. There have been a few times when he could not deny it. We were down stairs one night, the kids were asleep in bed, I was on the computer and Jessey was watching a movie. We both heard someone knock on our front door. Jessey got up to answer it, but there was no one there, it was about eleven o'clock at night, so I knew there would not be anyone there. Over the next few nights, I kept seeing a man's face in the window on the front door; he did not look like he was out side the door, but inside, sort of like a reflection. No matter how many times I looked out side, there was never anyone there.

Lying in bed another night, Jess and I heard the children playing in the playroom, he told me to go get them back to bed, but they were already in bed. Jessey just shrugged it off, but he could not deny hearing it, after all, he had sent me in there.

He tries hard to explain where these noises are coming from, and some of his reasons are just not likely. It is an old house, so the walking I hear up the stairs is just the old house and hardwood floors settling. The man I saw on the stairs was in my imagination, and the children's voices we have both heard, was a TV (that was not on), the lights turning on and off, is just faulty wiring or bulbs, and the kids' toys turning on and off is the batteries dying. Therefore, in his point of view, all these things happening simultaneously are completely normal.

More events occur on almost a nightly basis, but it is when they happen in broad day light that I get confused. Staying home from work one-day sick, Jessey had taken the boys to the sitters so that I could get some rest. Mid-afternoon sometime, I went to the kitchen to get a bit of lunch. I did not feel right, the type of feeling that you get, when someone is staring you right in the face a few inches from your nose yelling at you. I got a chill up my spine, left my lunch on the counter and went back to my bedroom. I shut the door and called Jessey, I just wanted someone to talk to, so I did not feel alone. Since he was at work, he really could not talk. All through the day, I heard noises, throughout my house. I stayed in my room, with the TV turned way up and the fan on high, to drown out the noises. Shortly before Jessey's return home from work, I heard the hinges on the door creaking, I looked up to see the door standing partially open. I kept my eye on it for a moment, and then decided I had just not shut it all the way. I looked away, and heard it again, I looked up and the door was open more. I kept checking and re-checking the door, and every time I looked at it, it would stop moving. This bothered me so much that I called Jessey again and harassed him to come home. Good thing was he was really close to home when I called him; it only took a few minutes for him to get there.

One night, I swore I heard the sound of little tiny feet race past my bedroom door, I opened the door to find out what it was, and I saw no one. Right before I closed the door again, I heard someone stammering up the stairs. I looked to find my oldest son Anthony walking up to me. He had begun a long battle with sleepwalking. He did not even notice that he had been down stairs in the dark of night with no lights on in the house.

This happened a few more times before I started sleeping with my door open, which seems to help, because he just walks into our room. It is scary enough that my child is sleep walking, but thinking that he would be doing this going down the stairs in the middle of the night. I know there is nothing paranormal about sleep walking, but that is the reason that my bedroom door does not open anymore at night. I leave it open for him, just incase it continues.

Recently our central air unit went out, the fan motor burned up or something, it would be a few days, if not weeks before it could be fixed. It was mid-summer, with ninety-degree temperatures and higher. To avoid sweating at night, we all camped out in the living room where we had a box fan in the window and a ceiling fan on high. My sleepless nights continued.

The living room has pocket doors on both sides of it, we closed them at night to keep one room cool and not worry about the rest of the house, as there was not much else we could do. We needed to keep at least one room cool so we could sleep at night. I however, never really got the chance. Still every night, now being down stairs, I heard what was going on down here from a closer perspective.

I also recall one night being up very late because of the noises that came from above where I was laying. This would be the kids' playroom. Thumping, rattling, footsteps, and voices. At times sounding as though the ceiling fan were going to come down on our heads. I turned it off and listened but it did not stop. I heard rustling outside my window, that I thought could be a raccoon or a cat, but as I checked out the window, in the luminous light coming from the streetlights, I found no animal or person out there.

The night of August 29th really got to me. It was 2 nights after my investigation in Marion Ohio, with the company of a great paranormal group called, Springfield Ghost Hunters; I was sitting in my bedroom catching up on my soap that I missed that day. When it was over, I was flipping through channels when I noticed that the box fan in my window kept slowing down, and speeding up. I got up to check it out, and the settings were all messed up. Low was High, High was low, and med was off. I could not figure it out, so I just decided it would fix it's self, or I would unplug it. I got the feeling someone was standing behind me, and I turned around, there was no one there, I went back to look at the fan again, only this time grabbing my digital camera, from the side of my bed. I kept turning the fan on and off, and then I felt it again, only closer. I quickly whipped around and snapped a photo. In the shot, you can clearly see two orbs shooting out the bedroom door. I had been seeing these balls of light all day long around the house and thought that it was just my eyes or something. Now I know it was not. I went down stairs and told my boyfriend about the fan, then showed him the picture; he raised his eyebrow to it. He said there could be something to that, if I had been seeing them all day. On my way back up the stairs, it was dark, a bit past midnight, I felt as though my foot was kicked out from under me, and I fell up the stairs. I hurt my little toe and the side of my foot. I concluded that they are getting sick of me trying to get proof that they are here.

Well, with the recorders and constantly snapping pictures. I did set up a recorder in the kid's play room one night, and captured a conversation between my oldest child, talking in his sleep, an unknown man's voice and another child, that wasn't his brother. You can clearly hear my oldest saying 'good, good' a few times, but between his 'goods' you can hear a mans voice that is difficult to make out, and a little girls voice, also difficult to make out. Unfortunately, those are the only two pieces of evidence that I have captured living here. It is enough to prove to the soon to be sister group of Southern New England Paranormal, Springfield Ghost Hunters, that there is something there.

As I sit here now writing all of this down in my laptop computer, I can feel eyes burrowing the back of my head, I can feel a 'cool spot' behind me, though there is no air vent or fan running. It is daytime out now, the sun is shining through the thick clouds and there are my children and Jessey walking about, and playing.

I can see a shadow out the corner of my eye from time to time as I glance around this empty dinning room area. The bunny eating her Alfalfa inside her cage just inside the living room, the dog asleep in the kitchen and the cat asleep upstairs, I know there is not someone standing behind me in the flesh, but maybe in another form.

The newest events that I have been experiencing are I finally saw a shadow figure of one of the little girls; she was darting into the kid's playroom. Phantom smells, like something cooking in my kitchen that smells good.

Last night I was hit, as I lay in my bed ready for the night I had been talking to Jessey about the possibility of moving far away from here, such as a different state, I went to bed leaving Jessey down stairs watching TV. I felt and heard the slap on my arm, I rolled over and I heard what sounded like some type of rustling, newspapers that my children had scattered around my bedroom that I had not picked up. I looked around and saw nothing. The underside of my forearm still hurting, I looked at it, and continued looking around my dark room, with a bit of light shining in from the cracked door, I saw no shadow, just the newspapers dropping back down on the floor. I got up, cleaned the newspapers up, and threw them in the trash.

I lay back down and took a deep breath, I stretched out my forearm and covered back up, for the next few minutes, I heard what sounded like the sound of little bare feet running up and down the hard wood floor hallway, and in and out of my bedroom. I kept looking around, snapping photos with my digital camera, and got nothing.

I finally fell asleep a little after midnight, and was awakened once more during the night, by some banging noises going on in the kids' playroom. I walked around the upstairs and found nothing. The disturbances continued all through the night into the wee morning hours. I went down stairs and turned on the television. During some of the day light hours I heard all sorts of noises coming from upstairs, as if a child were throwing a temper fit. Throwing things, and slamming doors. Some of these sounded like someone had broken into the house at times. I am a very paranoid person, and that was the first thing that came to mind. Not paranormal, not animals, an intruder. I grabbed a knife from the kitchen counter, and wandered up to the playroom, looking in closets, behind doors, in closed off bedrooms, and under beds. I did not find anything that I could use the knife against, so that proved to be a futile effort.

I am not scared of anything in this house, even though I was hit last night. It did not leave a mark at all, just a sore spot, which still at this time I can feel it, just not see it.

We were talking about the move, we are moving from this house soon, Jessey had gone down stairs to watch TV and I was ready for bed. I heard some paper rustling near my bed, but blew it off. Then I felt and heard a hard slap on my right forearm. I heard what sounded like little bare feet running across the wood floor in my bedroom. I swiftly sat up and looked around but there was no one there. I walked out of my room across the hall to the boy's room, and they were fast asleep. I do not think the little girl wants us to leave and she was just showing her feelings about it.

It has been rather quiet lately in my house, we are moving really soon and I do not know if that has something to do with it. I have only heard a few things, like a sort of shuffling noise on my bedroom floor a few times, but nothing that made me take too much notice.

We are going to be out of this house by the holidays, and then this house will be someone else's problem.

Kristy Hinkle

THE DAY JOB

After leaving the bar to take a job in a warehouse, I thought that it was all over.

It was a new building, and there had not been any traumatic deaths in the place, or during construction of it.

I had not been there long before I started getting the feeling of being watched, given that I worked with nearly two hundred others in there, I figured it could be coming from anywhere.

After being there for nearly two years, I was moved to a different location in the building. Working at a computer with my back to only one person, I was very comfortable there.

It was not long after that I started feeling a horrible feeling that someone was standing behind me. I knew there was Brian back there, but when I turned around, he was working and not close to me, and several times, he was not there at all.

After feeling what was strange to even me, instead of what is normally called a 'cold spot', it was a 'hot spot' the front of my body would be fine, but my back would feel as though there was a sun lamp behind me. It was so hot one time that I thought, it was burning me. At that point, I went to my friend Megan and asked her to come over to my work area. I did not tell her why, just asked her to stand in my spot for a minute, she agreed, but looked at me as if I was nuts, until she stood there, it only took a second for her to feel it too. She jumped back and yelled, what the hell is that? I answered that I did not know, and that got Brian's attention. He walked over, not realizing that he was walking right into the affected area, he stopped in his tracks. He yelled, what was that. He put his hand out into the hot spot and waved it back and fourth. He was as dumbfounded as Megan and I were. I just looked at them both, and told them that we were not alone in this place. Megan had never had any sort of experience before that, or since, but I have.

Later in the year, I was walking through the building when I saw a man in a red shirt, which did not look familiar, I went to smile at him, and he was gone. This startled me and I ran to Brian. I told him what I had seen and he was shocked as well, he wanted to know why he could not see these things, and I just told him he needed to open up to it.

Again later, I was walking down the stairs, at the end of the stairs up just high, enough to block view there is a conveyor belt, under it I saw legs walking, I followed them with my eyes, and started walking down the stairs, when I got to the bottom I saw the legs and there was no upper half. It was just legs, and then it was gone.

I soon started seeing him everywhere, walking across the floor, and standing at my work section, and even going down to the lunchroom. I only worked there for a little more than three years, but I could not understand why I was the only one seeing things. There were things disappearing from lockers, and drawers, and things being moved. We would always blame it on the other shifts, but they all insisted they had nothing to do with it.

I know I am not the only person who had experienced things in this place, but no one else would come forward.

I have asked around and no one will admit to anything. I do not know why some people will not talk, but they just will not.

There was only one person who did ever admit to seeing anything and she did not stay there long. She saw something one time when she was working, she told me all about it, and she described the same thing I had seen with the red shirt, and everything. She did not stay long, as she was from a temporary agency and after complaining about the behavior of a few full time employees she was not brought back, by company orders. I wish I could talk to her again, but I was unable to locate her for comment.

Kristy Hinkle

THE MARION INVESTIGATION

A two-part investigation of a private residence, in Marion Ohio.

(Photograph by, Kristy Hinkle)

This is a story told by my oldest sister Kelly, and her family. Husband Russ, and step children Andy, Alex and Amy.

I am a paranormal investigator, by trade. One day I was pulled aside by my sister Kelly and her husband Russ. They had an issue with the house that they had just purchased a few months before. Kelly has always considered herself a very sensitive person. However, this house was not triggering any feelings in her. Her husband was the one having problems with it.

A few months after moving in, when Kelly was working the night shift, Russ heard some voices coming from the living room; He went down stairs, as he knew his children were at their mother's house. The voices sounded like kids though. When he got down there, no one was there. He shrugged it off, as being neighbor kids running the streets at night, and went back to bed. He did not sleep much that night, when he got into bed and hunkered down, he felt the bed shake as though someone were climbing in bed with him. He swore he could feel a cool breath on his neck. This scared him; he is not one who typically believes in these sorts of things.

A few nights later, he was going into the bathroom, and he ran face to face with a man standing just out side the door. This was the first apparition in this home, and there were a few more to come. This is where the investigation will play a roll in this story, as I was accompanied by a local group called Springfield Ghost Hunters Society, to look into this case.

During a phone interview with the family I discovered that their daughter Amy, had experienced something in the upstairs hall as well, she claimed to have seen a white mass, floating at the top of the stairs a few feet off the ground, the oldest son Andy, says he hears a girl calling to him in his room. The middle child Alex will not admit to anything, however, he lived in the house longer than the other two, and decided to move in with his mom again, unexpectedly.

Russ has also posed a claim of a night, when Kelly and Russ got into an argument, after Kelly went down stairs, Russ claims the bed in their room started to shake vigorously as though it were kicked.

I arrived at the home in question on Saturday, August 26th, 2006. A local Ohio group called Springfield Ghost Hunters Society joined me.

On my initial go over of the house, I took some out side pictures for my records.

When the group arrived, we went on the tour of the place, and were given specifics of where things were happening to this family.

Many questions were raised about my abilities as a psychic, and I casually explained that I managed to keep them under control most the time, and I had them blocked at the initial walk through. We went into the basement where we were shown the different rooms in this old early 1900's home. When I opened the coal room door, I leaned over, flipped the light switch, and walked away. The head of the group, Kathy hollered for me. I walked over to her and found the investigator in training, John, was running EMF (Electro Magnetic Field) in the coal room. Kathy explained that she had had a vision of some sort, she saw in her head a little girl playing tea party. She described the little girl from her hair to her teddy bear. When the EMF (Electro Magnetic Field) was taken in there and John got a high spike at the spot where Kathy had seen the little girl playing, in her mind. She had gotten a psychic impression, she claims not to be a psychic, and I think everyone has it in them, it just chooses it is moments to make its presence known.

Upon entering the room and searching around on the

floor near the remnants of an old small table I found a very old glass baby doll bottle, it said Even Flo on the side of it, next to it I found a little girls plastic hair barrette also buried in the rubble of the old table.

As I stood facing the others talking about the baby bottle, I felt like someone was standing ridiculously close to me, I turned around and told them that I felt like there was someone behind me, John ran the EMF (Electro Magnetic Field) on my back and got another spike of energy. As suddenly as it appeared, it was gone.

In another part of the basement, Kathy and I were taking some pictures with our digital cameras when both of our screens went out. We could still take pictures but the screens were not working. Hers came back on. Mine stayed off for a while, then finally I got it back on, but it did not last long. I went up stairs and it worked again, I found it odd, and hoped that I had not broken it. Kathy reassured me that it happens a lot with digital cameras, because of the energy a spirit needs to do certain things.

Later on during the investigating part of it, I was sitting in the homeowner's bedroom talking with Dave and Dorothy about some friends of mine and a tour I took of a prison in West Virginia when suddenly I heard a shh sound, and stopped the conversation. I asked them if they heard it and they said no. I was the only one who had heard it. We sat and listened again, and started asking questions, I had a tape recorder going, but it stopped during our questioning and I had forgotten to bring a new tape with me to the bedroom. I heard the sound again, but no one else did.

When we had finished in that room, we went into another bedroom. Unfortunately, there were too many outside noises to get any good recordings.

We wrapped it up at around midnight, and I talked to

the homeowners briefly about certain things, being careful not to reveal it all before, I had time to go over the rest of the tapes, and pictures.

After looking at the photos on my computer, and listening to the tapes I found a few pieces of evidence. A photograph that I had taken of the out side of the house just for my own records ended up having an image in a window. A person's face that did not appear to be a reflection of anyone that was in the shot. They were also too far to the side to have been reflecting in that window. I found a few pictures of orbs, little balls of light appearing in a photograph. No guarantee of a haunting, but it is proof that there is energy, whether natural or not.

I also captured two EVP's, (Electro Voice Phenomenon) I caught the wheezy breath from the master bedroom on there and also there was one time I allowed Kelly, the homeowner, to take my recorder up to her room with her, and she asked if they could tell us who they were, and you can clearly hear a voice say, 'no'.

We do plan on going back there, sometime in the near future, though we did catch something, we did not catch enough to declare the place haunted. We can freely say though, that there is some type of paranormal activity there.

I think that one of the best things to come out of this case is the fact that I made a few new friends. Kathy, Dave, Dorothy, and John, From the Springfield Ghost Hunters. Not to mention they invited me to go on another case with them to a haunted mansion here in Ohio. If something happens there, I promise you will know about it!

Kristy Hinkle

With personal thanks to Springfield Ghost Hunters Society, of Springfield Ohio.

Kathy Wolboldt
John Middleton
Dave Frevert
Dorothy Frevert

On October 14th 2006, a second investigation was conducted with the assistance of Southern Ohio Paranormal Research. During this investigation, we had a few new investigators with us, and they did a great job. I was partnered up with Rainie this time around, and we were teased about how we kept giggling. We enjoyed each other's company and found many things to talk about. As we sat at the beginning of the investigation in the upstairs bedrooms, we noticed of course, that there was a lot of background noise, coming from out side, and down stairs. We conducted our part of the investigation starting in the child's room where the residents of this house had spotted the apparition. We did not have any experiences in this room, so we moved on to the next. The master bedroom was a bit more exciting, we sat asking questions running EVP's on the room, and chatting. As I remembered from the first investigation, they did not like it when I talked. I was shh'd on the first investigation of this house, when I was talking to Dorothy and Dave.

As we sat, there not much time passed until we started hearing noises. We listened for a bit and heard things like a door latching shut. It did not sound like the door on the master bedroom, but like the door on the room, we had just been in. The only problem with that was that the door on the child's bedroom did not latch. I walked to the bedroom door and looked out and there was no one there, and the door to the child's room was open, the way we had left it. I went back in and shut the door, sat back down on the bed with Rainie, and continued our investigation. We kept hearing what sounded like a door latching, and then it got a little more exciting. We heard footsteps coming up the stairs, and then a door latch. I jumped up and went to look at the door, and nothing. No one was there again and the door was still open to the child's bedroom. We asked others if they had come up the stairs and none of them had. We relayed our experiences to the others in the group as they shared theirs. In the basement, they had had a great experience with some sounds of footsteps and sand dropping on the ground near their feet. It was our turn to venture into the basement, we were hesitant about going into the basement, neither one of us were thrilled about basements, but in the interest of the investigation we went and did our jobs. We personally had no experiences down there, but did not let that stop us. We went back upstairs it was our turn on the main floor. This time we were doing fine but still had nothing going on as we sat in the spare room on the first floor.

Then we started getting cold in there, and the coldest spot ended up being next to my leg. My leg and left side got cold; Rainie put her hand over there and felt it too. Then we started hearing someone knock on the bedroom door, thinking it was a member of the group, we instinctively said come in. We got no answer so we said, hello, come on in. Still we got nothing, we opened the door, and sure enough, no one was there.

The others had reported a banging noise that the homeowner had complained about before the investigation. The homeowner was relieved that someone else had heard the same things that she and her family had been hearing. She was glad that someone else had heard it too; she did not feel crazy anymore.

We wrapped up the investigation late, around one thirty or later, but we had all felt that the investigation went great, and we had enough to work with. Besides, the activity had started slowing down to a minimum so we headed out.

As for evidence collected, we only managed to capture EVP's this go round, and some of them were quite frightening.

One you can hear a little girl saying, 'She knows' or 'He knows' another one you can hear a mangled voice and cannot really make out what is being said, and still another one was terrifying just the thought. The voice had mechanical disturbances in it, and says something to the effect of "God Damn you, Fucking Bitch"

This is disturbing, but we do not know whom this voice was talking to.

I am very pleased with this investigation, and just in my personal opinion with the experiences that we had there, I am willing to label this house haunted finally.

For round two of the Marion investigation I would like to thank Southern Ohio Paranormal Research for accompanying me on this one. Those who drove three or more hours to get to the investigation site.

James
Brian
Rainie
Jessica
Kevin

THE FLAGSTAFF HOUSE

By Marie Cipriano

(Picture provided by, Marie Cipriano)

This is a story that has a genuine historical background. In Windham County, there is a residence, where George Washington had stopped at on a warm day, for some water from the well.

This area of Thompson Connecticut had very few established properties in those days, a restaurant called Vernon Stiles, a few barns and the Flagstaff House. This at that time had been a woman's birthing center. George Washington had to travel three miles north of Vernon Stiles to reach the Flagstaff House.

Flagstaff House is now a historical landmark and needs to be preserved as such, this house requires paint from only one location, being as it is a historical landmark, Sturbridge Village is the only place that has the paint required to maintain the property. The paint outside is made from pure grain, and the blue paint on the inside walls are made from Blueberries. This house dates back to Seventeen hundred, Thirty-Two.

As a young girl, I lived in this house. This is what happened to me.

Late one night in the early Nineteen Eighties as I lay sleeping soundly in my bed, I had a frightening experience. My bed faced the only window in this room, I was awakened by the sound of loud growling near my window, I can only stress that this sound did not sound like any human or animal that I had ever heard, the noise was coming from outside my window.

I lay there still as a board and did not move for several minutes. After that long period, the noise did not stop; I picked up my head to look at the window. What I saw was not human, or animal. To this day, it still gives me chills to think about it. I believe this is why I have not spoken of this until now.

There was a creature with his face pressed up against my window screen, as if trying to get into my bedroom. With its head pressed directly into my screen I could not make out any facial features, all I could tell was that it had sort of a dog type head, with its claws attached to my screen; its eyes were hypnotizing and horrifying. It had to be more than six feet tall, as my bedroom window was more than five feet off the ground and there was nothing under the window, which could have been used as a stool.

I tried to climb out of my bed slowly, I thought I would not be noticed, but the creature's eyes were staring at me in such a way they followed my every move, I screamed loudly for my parents.

As I turned back to the window I saw the creature backing away from the window, I kept watching its shadow as it left, I was still screaming, and then it was gone. My parents still to this day believe it was my imagination, but for those of you out there who know what I am talking about, you know this was not a dream.

As far as I know, no one has reported anything similar to this creature anywhere in or around the area.

Marie Cipriano

THE GRIM REAPER

One hot summer day, during rush hour traffic, the highway was packed full and at a dead stop. She thought there had to be an auto accident up ahead somewhere. She and my dad were sitting in traffic, moving only inches at a time, and getting frustrated. As they neared an overpass up ahead, she saw someone in the road, walking around the cars. He was a tall man with a black large brimmed hat and a long black heavy coat.

Thinking to herself that this was the reason for the stopped traffic, she starts yelling at him to get out of the road, out the open window. He did not look at her, or even respond to her yelling, he just kept walking around the highway.

Finally, my dad asked whom she was yelling at; she answered him and pointed to the man walking in the middle of the street. He answered that he did not see anyone up there, and told her she was seeing things.

She kept her eyes on this strange man, only seeing a profile view of his face all the way down the road. They crept slowly passed him, at under two miles and hour in the slow traffic, until they were finally past him by about two car lengths, when he vanished.

Unsure of what she had actually seen, she rubbed her eyes, and looked back. He was nowhere to be found.

To this day, my mother continues to see strange people that my dad cannot see. She makes sure she is really seeing something by continually asking if that person is really standing there or not. Many times, he cannot see what, or whom she is seeing.

This is a family trait that I seem to have inherited from her; I see things many times, which my boyfriend cannot see.

Kristy Hinkle

JONATHAN FROM ALABAMA

This came to me from Jonathan in Alabama.

(Photo Courtesy of Jonathan from Alabama)

(Look closely at this window)

When Jonathan was seventeen years old, he and his parents moved into an old Victorian style home, built in 1910, in Florence Alabama.

It had a reputation for being haunted; it was an old white house, with pink shutters, which was in good repair given its age. The house looked creepy from the street, especially after the sun went down.

Their real estate agent joked about the two little girls said to haunt the house, She claimed that they along with their parents had perished in a car accident in the 1930's or 40's.

It is said that the little girls came back to the home for

their dolls.

Jonathan's first experience came just days after moving into the home. He was home alone during the day while his parents worked, on a trip down the shadowy hall he passed his parents open bedroom door, where he heard audible men's voices coming from inside. It sounded as though there were someone inside the room carrying on a conversation, He could not make out what they were saying. He stood outside the open door for a few moments listening to the muffled voices, until they disappeared.

At the age of seventeen, Jonathan was more curious than scared. He wondered repeatedly if the house truly was haunted.

The second and last experience for Jonathan came at night, as he lay in his bed. He did not feel comfortable that night and had trouble sleeping, when he heard a single footstep in the hall near his bedroom door.

Any number of things could explain this; however, Jonathan believes it was a footstep. Possibly from one of the little girls who are said to haunt this old Victorian, in Florence Alabama.

Ths experience has been with Jonathan for many years, and was glad to finally, talk about it to someone. I am glad to write it down for him, as even if they are small in size, any experience can be big and memorable to the individual that it happens to.

PHANTOM CAR

Have you ever wondered what the deal is with Phantom Cars? You are driving down the road one night, and you see headlights in your rearview mirror one moment, and the next they are gone.

    I have had such an encounter, I was driving to a gas station before work one day around four in the morning, the darkness surrounded the car, so thick that the head lights barely lit the road, a street that took you through a wooded area, no houses around, no streetlights to light the way.

    Suddenly coming up behind me fast was a car with its bright lights on. I was blinded, as they got right on the tail of my car; I adjusted my mirrors to get their lights out of my eyes as I slowed to a stop at the stop sign up ahead. I was next to a cemetery, that many times had cars plummet through the fence and often taken out several old headstones and small trees. The road was curvy and the cemetery was at the end of a sharp curve next to the stop sign. I had never personally witnessed any crashes there but I had seen the after math, with the fence lying on the ground. There used to be a huge tree there, but after it had been hit many times, the care takers cut it down, making the grave markers more susceptible to the on-coming cars.

    I looked behind me as this car did not appear to be

stopping, I braced for impact but there would not be one. The car had vanished upon what should have been an immanent crash to the back of my car. There was no possible explanation for its disappearance, there were no driveways for it to turn into and there was no way it would not have hit me, it was a few feet away from my car. I sat in my car looking around for a few minutes to make sure my eyes were not playing tricks on me, and then I proceeded to the gas station. I told the gas station attendant, whom I knew, about the event and he informed me that I am not the only person to mention this. He claimed that someone saw the same thing just the morning before, and he himself had seen it too on his way into work a few times before. He lived near me so he took the same roads as I did to get to the gas station.

I could not believe it, I had read about Phantom Cars a few times on the internet, but never in all my life thought for a second that I would personally see one, I had never thought it was possible.

After that morning, ever time I drove down that road in the dark, I would be looking out for that Phantom Car. I have not seen it since, but I look forward to possibly seeing it again.

Kristy Hinkle

PROSPECT PLACE MANSION INVESTIGATION

(Photographs by Kristy Hinkle)

Prospect Place Mansion located just out side of Dresden Ohio, was built in eighteen fifty six, by a man named George W. Adams, it is now a learning center with a haunted past.

Once played the roll of a station on the Underground Railroad, the mansion was a sign of hope, as well as a new life for fugitive slaves traveling up the river towards freedom.

George Adams built the first working flour mill in the area, saving people a long trip to Columbus.

Hiding fugitive slaves was a dangerous business; bounty hunters came looking for slaves at the Adams property many times, one or more is believed to have been killed by George Adams' stable hands. Tried for crimes against god, and convicted by the stable hands; sentenced to death by hanging in the large 3-story barn.

A young girl about twenty-one years old fell to her death from a balcony after she fell ill and lost her balance at the railing. The family was unable to bury her in the winter months due to the frozen ground; her body was stored in the cool room awaiting burial in the spring.

Others, who lost their lives there, included one fugitive slave woman who arrived at the home with a head injury, and died while in their care.

There are several spirits believed to reside in the mansion, such as Mary Elizabeth, second wife to George W. Adams, Constance daughter of William and Anna Cox, possibly more fugitive slaves, a little girl and her mother in the servant's quarters. William Cox is said to reside in the ballroom, along with several others who like to dance to music, and the bounty hunter who still resides in the barn.

Prospect Place stood empty for nearly thirty years giving the local teenagers and vandals plenty of time to destroy the once beautiful mansion on the hill. Time and weather also took its toll on the mansion; Prospect Place is now in the process of restoration, efforts by the current living descendant George J. Adams. Who is doing a marvelous job restoring the property to its former glory.

I had the opportunity to investigate this home with two paranormal groups on Saturday September 9, Two Thousand and six, Springfield Ghost Hunters Society out of Springfield Ohio, and Southern Ohio Paranormal Research out of Cincinnati Ohio. Two great groups of people; I was one of ten people on this case.

The combination of three research groups these days is rare, and foreboding as many other groups would respond, but we enjoy each other's company and had a great time working together on this project.

Prospect Place Mansion is very large and requires a large group of people to investigate it. Kathy Wolboldt from Springfield Ghost Hunters Society invited me along, to help.

During the initial walk through of the mansion, in Mary Elizabeth's bedroom, I was feeling nervous and jumpy sort of, like I wanted to or needed to run. In the ballroom after the sun had set, we were going through listening to accounts of activity and experiences from our guide, I walked over next to Kathy and before I could get my footing, I felt as though someone shoved me in to a corner. Which I later found out was the corner in which Satanists had performed animal sacrifices in the nineteen eighties. I did not feel the pressure of any hands, but it was as though an unseen force was forcing me back into that corner.

When we went out on our own, I stopped feeling anything. I did not feel anxious anymore, I did at one time hear what sounded like music playing in the ballroom, but was unable to catch this on my recorder or find a source for it. That was it for my experiences through the night. However, members from the group Southern Ohio Paranormal Research did have several experiences.

Brandon Acus had been plagued all night long with

several types of experiences; this is what he told me about this investigation.

To start off the night, on the Servants Quarters balcony he says he felt as though he were being watched so intently that it was as if someone were burning their glare into the back of his skull. He leaned over to James and explained what he had been feeling, and asked him to take a few pictures of him. By the time James was ready to take the pictures the feeling was gone.

Following the initial tour, they pulled the group together and described what he had felt on the balcony. This had proven good information at another home they had investigated and he had had the same experience. They ended up getting plenty of activity from one room where Brandon had his feeling.

After doing some research in the barn, he and Brian ventured up to the servants quarters to investigate. They began their investigation in the washroom, the room overlooking the balcony where he had been standing when he had his feeling of being watched.

They began EVP (electro voice phenomenon) work in the wash room, for several minutes they listened and waited, asked questions and waited some more. After nearly five minutes, something caught Brandon's eye, running into the servant's room. They gave chase, ending up in the upstairs kitchen in the servant's quarters, where they continued their investigation. They ran video in two rooms, when Brandons feeling of being watched returned, Brian and Brandon started doing some simple questioning. He got the feeling that it was coming from one corner of the room; they started asking for signs of a presence, such as a noise or something to that effect. Indeed, they got their response. Shortly following this request, they started hearing scratching and thumping noises, he asked if he could sit near them in the corner, after getting no response he sat anyways.

The next ten to fifteen minutes passed with some basic questioning, and he asked if it could brush his arm, this question was followed by a cool sensation touching the back of his hand which was quickly followed up with a rustling back in the corner, that had disturbed some pieces of wood that were propped up there. At that point Brandon scooted his chair back away from the corner; he started getting the feeling of being startled and a slight panic. He took the chair and moved it to the center of the room, the questioning continued, but the feeling of being watched was still there. Soon after he moved the chair to the center of the room, he felt as though he wanted to vomit, then the feelings were as though he needed to or was being pushed to leave the room. They asked if they were being told to leave and they got a response with the moving of the wood and the shuffling in the corner of the room again. They packed up their items, Brandon still feeling very sick and teary eyed, they left the mansion.

Later during the investigation, the tour guide had loaned her divining rods to the members of Southern Ohio Paranormal Research. I later joined them to witness how these actually work; I have never used them before, and am unsure if I will use them in the future. They experimented with them for a long while in the servants quarters and then again in the ballroom, where we also attempted Table Tipping, another form of contact that I do not subscribe to. It did prove to be quite interesting, though.

Several of us watched as the tour guide along with, Kathy Wolbodlt from Springfield Ghost Hunters Society, Brian Klein, and Brandon Acus from Southern Ohio Paranormal Research, participated in a Table Tipping experiment.

As they went ahead with that experiment, the rest of us went to wonder about the mansion talking and looking around. Three of us, Niki Bailey, James Bell and me returned to check in with them and we stood there for a brief moment watching the event on a night vision, camera screen, we watched as they asked questions and as the table levitated off the ground. The angle we had from the night vision camera was directly under the table from the side. We could see with that camera every leg, and finger, hoping to catch someone helping the table along. We were successful in only finding the table lifting from the floor on its own as far as we could tell.

We took our leave and went back out in the mansion, looking in the different rooms, and wondering the second floor.

We wondered into the servant's quarters where James Bell, described the events that had taken place with his group member Brandon Acus in the kitchen area.

We returned at the end of the Table Tipping experiment, and gathered as a large group out side to discuss the results.

I was still uncertain about the findings, as the group had spent so much time up there with these sorts of experiments that were not scientific at all, I do however believe that you must give everything a fair chance. I still do not subscribe to it at all and will not put myself in the position to risk any kind of exposure like that; I will not leave my self open like that.

As we all went our separate ways again, in small groups of two's and three's I did not witness anything out of the ordinary. I carried on several conversations about many different events in the mansion; we talked about its history and the people who died there.

We gathered as a group one last time, in the gentleman's parlor to view the two videos of the Table Tipping experiment. As far as that goes, I was only impressed with the results from one angle, and the fact that

I trust each member of both groups to be completely honest with the rest of us. After James, Niki and I had left the Ball Room, so did the tour guide, three were left with the table, and it kept moving, this I was happy with. We could not accuse someone who was no longer in the room. All we have is our trust of the other group members, to be honest and not play games with experiments.

After my initial review of the evidence that I had collected on an Analog recorder and my digital camera, I noticed that all of the tapes I had gone through in the mansion were ruined. There was only garble on them, I tried and tried to get them to play. I finally succeeded and did manage to get one strange EVP; what sounded like a little girl going through the alphabet. She simply said 'E', flat out. I also went back through my two hundred plus photographs on my computer, lightening them up as I went. I did catch some strange photographs, but we were able to rule out most of them, only one is still unexplained. That is the one we are putting fourth as evidence. In addition, the others have sent me EVP recorded on digital recorders one being the same one as I got on my tape. Another sounds like, 'Oh I know', or 'all I know', one sounds like 'right' and yet another sounds like the biggest cliché 'Boo'. These were recorded by members of Springfield Ghost Hunters Society, and Southern Ohio Paranormal Research, these can be found as well as any pictures or videos, on the web pages for all three groups.

We have the video of the Table Tipping experiment, and the Divining Rods experiment and we are satisfied with that. As for other pictures, I have yet to receive word from some members of both groups as to what they may have captured.

My ruling of this place is that it is definitely haunted.

This is one photo I took during the investigation, in the basement of the Mansion, and is being used as evidence for all three of the groups involved in this investigation.

(Photograph by Kristy Hinkle, Sept. 9th 2006 investigation, Prospect Place Mansion)

    If you are ever in Ohio, around the Dresden way, you should stop in for a tour, and stay for an investigation. Get a room for the night maybe, and see what you encounter. Maybe Mary Elizabeth herself will visit your room, or maybe on a trip to the bathroom in the middle of the night you will encounter Constance Cox. You may spot a young servant girl and her mother, practicing the alphabet or working on the household chores, or maybe even see strange lights flickering from the barn windows. Take a night trip to the Ball Room to blow off some steam, dance the waltz and you may find yourself dancing with the spirit of William Cox, you never know until you try it!
    Watch from the balcony as the fog rolls in over the fields, while the hill around Prospect Place remains clear, with the full moon shining over head, it is truly a beautiful sight.

Prospect Place Mansion is located just a half mile north of Dresden Ohio, in Trinway.

I would like to thank those involved in this investigation.

Springfield Ghost Hunters Society;

Kathy Wolboldt
John Middleton
Dave Frevert
Dorothy Frevert
Niki Bailey

Southern Ohio Paranormal Research;

James Bell
Brian Klein
Brandon Acus
Lorain (Rainie) Mendleson

FORT GRISWOLD INVESTIGATION

On September 30th, 2006, for the first time, I was able to investigate with my own group, Southern New England Paranormal. The location opened up for us, was Fort Griswold Battlefield in New London Connecticut.

Upon our arrival to Fort Griswold, we made quick notations of the locations of dips in the ground, and rocks. Things that could cause injury to the members of our group. As we were given permission to do our investigation, it was up to us to try to keep it from being compromised.

Fort Griswold, an outdoor park closes at dark. To investigate this location you do need permission, and a contract in order to have access to the park after closing.

The ground is very uneven, there are many dips and rocks scattered around the ground. There is a pit, or fox hole that stretches the length of the hill. With an American flag perched on the top.

Many people died here during a struggle for the land, between the settlers and the British armies. There are a few outbuildings and one tunnel; and one door we did not have access to.

The stories here are not widely known, but the experiences we had at this location, we hope, will incite other investigators to go and look. Remember, you need permission before entering the park after the sun sets.

Over looking the harbor, where ships come and go, surrounded by houses on the other three sides. We arrived at Fort Griswold, at around six thirty in the evening. After the park closed and after making our presence there known to the local police department.

During our initial walk through with the quickly disappearing sun light, we ran into a woman who claimed to be there as a rescuer. She gave off the worst vibe, every member of our group felt as though she were ready to verbally attack us. We explained to her that we were there to perform an investigation, and she explained that she was trying to get the restless souls to cross over. We instructed her to make her way towards the exit, as the park had closed and with a slight glare, she finally did make her way out. Other interruptions through the night did not stop our investigation, just prolonged it.

After the sun had completely set, we made our way back to the cars to gather more of our equipment. We were going to do this as simply as possible, due to the fact that it was an out door investigation, we were not comfortable setting all of our equipment out where we could not watch it closely.

We split into two groups of five, the first group Marie and I took 3 members with us. Group two consisted of five other members of the group. With our group heading to the top of the hills, and the other group headed to the bottom of the hills, we initiated our investigation, with minor equipment, such as EMF detectors, digital voice recorders, a video camera and many flashlights and digital cameras.

The first thing our group decided to check out was the tunnel, but as we approached the tunnel I felt as though we were being closely watched, and then started getting a sharp pain behind my right ear. Marie and I sent the other three members into the tunnel, as we walked down the hill to find out where it was coming from. As we got closer, the feeling of not being wanted got stronger. We went up the hill after deciding that we were not welcome down there, but the whole trip back we both felt like there was someone walking really closely behind us, we kept turning around, and snapping photos, but we could not get anything.

We informed the rest of the group of what we were feeling, and then we saw a black shadow, it appeared to duck into the ditch and run the other way. We gave chase and eventually lost it around a corner.

We were starting to get excited, as we felt like we were finally about to get something on film. Soon after, we saw another shadow, taking off down the ditch, but this time as we gave chase with the cameras, I felt something burning on my right shoulder. I described what I had felt, at the same time; one other member had the same experience, on the left side of her back. It was interesting to hear that we were having similar experiences and feelings at the same time.

She brought the EMF detector close to me as I went down; a very strong pain in my left side brought me to my knees. Nearly dropping the video camera and trying to catch my breath after the attack, the EMF was giving a reading of 8.5 high reading for being outside. I thought it was my flashlight, but when holding the EMF to the flashlight, we got a reading of 30.8 and higher, so it could not have come from the flashlight.

We had several experiences that were many feelings, but we had quite a few people reporting black shadows, and touches.

We thought we were getting very close to capturing actual evidence, but we seemed to always be a second too late.

During our break, Marie asked us if we still had any

pain where we had experienced them earlier, we told her yes, and she immediately lifted up our shirts to find on my shoulder blade, a bite mark. Clearly made by human type teeth.

We lifted the back of the other members shirt to find that she had welts, and scratch marks across her back. Upon close inspection of my side, we noticed that I had a red mark where I had felt as though I had been hit.

After a short break, our groups went to switch areas. The second group was hoping to have the same or similar experiences as our group had, but upon re-entering the park, we found a couple of teens who were not happy to have us inform them that they were not allowed in the park after sunset. They exited the park, only to sit next to our vehicles. With many of our personal belongings and some equipment not in use still in these cars, we were not happy that they were there. We ended up needing the assistance of the Groton Police Department.

They responded very quickly to our call, and were awesome at helping us deal with this problem. They also asked if they could come out after their shifts were over and we of course told them yes.

Shortly after eleven at night, the two women whose shift had ended came to join us in our hunt.

Prior to their arrival, after we were able to go back in to the investigation, the second group headed up the hills, and Marie and I took our group to the bottom of the hills.

We followed voices that we had heard around the structures to no avail. We were unable to catch anyone playing games with us, or even find where the voices were coming from. We gave up that chase and sat on the ground to relax and run some EVP work. Me and one other member both turned at the same time to see a black figure running off towards the trees to the left of us, but at that moment, Marie and another member saw a black shadow figure walking calmly to the right towards the hill. We all got up and took off running in response to a male voice calling for help. Unfortunately, when we did get to the top of the hill, we saw a few more teens cutting through the park. Another segment of our investigation interrupted. This time though, they did not leave, we could hear them laughing and giggling near the structures. Therefore, we wrapped up that portion of our investigation, called the other group to meet up, and went out of the park to wait for our guests.

Unfortunately, the immensely strong feeling of being watched was not subsiding as we stepped out of the gate. I walked over to where I thought we were being watched and started getting stomach cramps. I yelled into the dark for it to go away, that we were on break, not really knowing why I had done that, I called over two members to see if they too felt what I did, and their answer was yes. Though the feeling was less than it had been it was still there.

Group two reported no unusual experiences while they were at the top of the hills, but Marie decided she needed to smudge some of the grounds with one member of the group. As they did this, they started near the top of the hill, in the tunnel. While inside the tunnel, Marie reported feeling someone rushing up to her, face to face, which startled her. They got out of the tunnel, and made their way around, and back to the group where the women from the Groton Police department had joined us. We were recounting the stories of experiences we had been going through since the investigation started. They were very excited to get in there and see what it was all about.

We took them around, showing them where things had been the strongest, and giving Fort Griswold one final going over, we did not have anymore-serious experiences, but only one more person had been touched, and as we made our way up and around, we gave chase to one more black shadow figure. We failed to catch it, but we gave them a good run.

While we were trying to leave, we felt like we were being followed again, after snapping many photos, and getting several spikes on the EMF we made it to the entrance, and walked out. We were asked to go to the cemetery down the road by one of the women from the Groton Police department. Normally we would not go into cemeteries, but on this particular occasion, we decided to go. How often will you get a police escort to a cemetery at one in the morning?

As we arrived at the cemetery, we noticed a severe change in the atmosphere. Where at Fort Griswold, the wind was strong, cold and unsettling; at the cemetery, everything was calm and peaceful. It was right down the road from the fort, so there was no real reason for the dramatic change. We did not have many experiences there, one member says he saw a shadow duck behind a few tall head stones, but it was gone by the time he got there. We did not get any evidence from the cemetery but got a few from the fort.

One piece of evidence was discovered by accident. Even mistakes, like this one can produce amazing evidence.

When we were running up the hill attempting to find where the yelling was coming from, one member hit the wrong button on her digital camera, and instead of taking a photo, she started recording video. Realizing what she had done fairly quickly she snapped a photo, and stopped recording.

Upon playing back the video, we found that at the top of the hill, where the camera had been aimed, instead of the flag that is on top of the hill, there was a blazing fire. In the video, you can see the entire fire. Flames leaping into the air, and even sparks, floating up. In the photo that she snapped immediately following the accidental video, you can see the light from the fire.

There was no fire up there it is a public park, no fires are allowed there.

Going over some of the pictures on the digital cameras, we found a few interesting photos taken at the fort. One of which appears to have a few faces in it, between two very brightly lit orbs. One looks like a head floating next to a small fire. That one was discounted for the reason that it was too hard to clean up and make larger.

One of the hardest parts of being an investigator is having to throw out possible evidence just because there is too much dust in the photo, or because there is no way to make them clear enough to make out a real image. I hate to throw out possible evidence, but I will do what I have to do to protect the reputation of a great group. We do not want a lot of skepticism when it comes to our evidence. I will not put things out there, if I am not positive, they are absolute and real.

With all evidence that you may come across you will find someone out there who thinks they know how you faked it, or how it was created by normal situations, not paranormal ones. Those are some of the worst of the skeptics who cannot take a groups word or proof of anything. They refuse to see it for what it is, and insist on saying what they want it to be, regardless of the evidence. That is fine, everyone is entitled to his or her own opinions, but the only people who will really know the facts surrounding the event are those who were present at the time the evidence was captured. Not many people will take someone's word for it, even if they caught it on many different levels, such as, an EVP spike, as well as video and photographic proof.

The evidence that we found at Fort Griswold, can be ridiculed, and probably will be. Nevertheless, I will stand behind what we captured on tape, and in photos.

Investigators names were omitted for privacy

reasons. As the members who were on this investigation; other than Marie and myself are no longer with Southern New England Paranormal, nor are they affiliated with the group in any way.

BIGFOOT?

How many of you believe in such things as Bigfoot? I am not sure what to believe, I mean they have no real evidence to support their beliefs and I am no different, I can only attest to what I have seen.

One night on my way home from my parents house in Delaware County Ohio, I witnessed something odd. It was a dark night out, one of those nights when the darkness was so intense that your headlights even on the bright setting barely lit the road in front of you. Coming down a dark country road, driving slowly to watch for deer that may jump out from the tall wheat or cornfields on either side of the road I barely saw something running just out of the reach of my bright lights.

I slammed on my brakes as it paused in the road; it came just inside the light as it ran into the mature corn on the left of my car. It was tall and dark colored, I sat there at a stop watching as the corn husks slammed to the left and right of the large animal running through it. Until it was too far in that, I could no longer see the movement of the stalks. I did not know what to make of this, as I am no Crypto Zoologist. I slowly moved forward to head back home, brushing it off, as maybe a horse had gotten loose, even though it did not appear to be a horse. After all, I had not been able to see it very well due to the lack of light on the roadway. I did know that it was tall and darkly colored.

On my arrival home, I mentioned to Jessey that I had seen Bigfoot, sort of as a joke. Until I heard from a friend of, mine who lived on that road that a farmer, had sworn to have seen Bigfoot on the other side of that cornfield. He had a much better view of him, as it was his house back there on that side, and he had floodlights, to light up his yard.

The police department apparently told him and others who had made this same complaint that it was a loose Clydesdale horse, which had escaped its enclosure. The main concern we all had was that no one in the area owns any Clydesdale horses. They mainly have Arabians, Quarters or miniatures. I do not see how anyone can make this claim; there is no way to mistake a Clydesdale for a Bigfoot, which does not make any sense to me. I am not going to claim that it was a Bigfoot that I saw that night. I did not get a good enough view to say yes or no to that. I wish I had but unfortunately, I did not. It very well could have been a Clydesdale horse for all I know, or more believably a brown bear, as those have been sighted in that area many times before during the daylight hours. If perhaps it was a bear standing on its hind legs when the farmer saw it, maybe it could have been mistaken for a Bigfoot, I cannot make a size judgment, it was too far away for me to make that call. I do know, it was big, and it was not a deer.

Kristy Hinkle

INVESTIGATING TIPS

Information you should know before investigating.

By Marie Cipriano

Paranormal Investigating, like most jobs, you have to be in the right frame of mind, to achieve the best possible results. One of the most important things to remember in this field is to keep an open mind. If you cannot do this, then how can you get the best results from the unknown?

Next thing to look at is do you have the desire to do this type of work and a love for this type of work?

Most of the Paranormal Investigators, you meet are just people who love this work. They have a thirst for knowledge, and a desire to find the known.

Some of the basic equipment used is.

Flashlights
Compass
EMF Meter (Electro Magnetic Field)
Digital Thermal Thermometer
Digital Camera / 35mm Camera
Video Camera

Tape Recorder with external microphone
Computer; Laptop or desktop.

You can purchase a lot more high tech equipment along the way. If you are tight for money, you can scale it down a bit. You can use the basics to get you started.

Flash Lights
Recorder; digital or tape
Camera; Digital or 35mm

You can save money to purchase other items at a later time.

If you are just going to have fun, and investigate in your spare time, you just need the basics, However if you want to investigate for real, you will need further evidence to back up your claims. This is where the more high tech equipment comes in to play.

With these tools you will also have to learn some investigative techniques, also you will need to identify any type of evidence that you may collect, and learn to do the research of any property, and any claims made of Paranormal activity at the Investigation site.

One thing you must remember,

'Always get permission to investigate any property; this is for your own safety as well as keeping you on the right side of the law.'

It is a good idea to arrive at the property early enough to get a feel for the place you are investigating during the day light hours. Then arrive approximately 30 minutes before sunset to make sure nothing has changes since your last visit. Example:

If you were in a home or building during the day,

sometime after you left there maybe a new obstacle in the hall or in the way of a door or something on the stairs that you can trip on and get injured, this is also a good reason to carry flashlights at all times, avoid pets when walking.

A Paranormal Investigators reputation is very important, it is a challenging field and one of much skeptical criticism, if we stumble, we will fall.

Spirit Energy comes in many forms, you are looking for Apparitions, Vortices, noises, Phantom Smells, mists or fog type energy and 'cold spots'.

Some groups believe that 'orbs' are spirit energy, or proof of some type of haunting, well Southern New England Paranormal, looks at 'orbs' as just energy, normal or paranormal, it does not matter, we will not submit orb activity as any type of paranormal proof.

Digital Camera vs. 35 mm

There are many factors in choosing which camera is for you. At S.N.E.P., we use both.

The positives of using Digital is you can see right away if you caught something, you can download it to your computer for a better look, and you can delete anything you do not need. The positives of using a 35 mm camera, you will have a negative to show you did not mess with the picture using a digital editor program.

When using a digital camera, take more than one photo of the same angle, and from different angles as well, you can make comparison shots, this will support your first spirit energy photo.

Most Paranormal groups have certain standards that we must abide by; you can read about ours on the S.N.E.P. Web site. This should help answer many questions that some people will inevitably have about your photos.

Example;

"Was anyone smoking, that caused this fog?"

"We do not smoke during investigations." Therefore, this would not be possible.

You can go to many Investigative group sites to look up their Code of Conduct. This will help you better understand their process of investigating. Please go to the sites of reputable groups.

Some out there that are so far out in left field, one way to tell is look at their investigations page. If they spend all their time in cemeteries, and not doing real locations like homes, buildings, and such, they are not a reputable group.

You want to find a group that has experience in real investigating. Not just walking through a cemetery or dark woods in the middle of the night with flashlights and cameras.

When you have done your research on a site that you were called in on, and you have followed procedure, walk through, and interviews.

Take your initial photos during daylight hours to substantiate the investigation. You always want to have those available if you are asked for them.

Now, if you found a place you would like to investigate, and you were not called in by the owner, you will need to do some research on this place, and obtain permission to investigate it. Not everyone is up for allowing you do conduct investigations, if you are told no, then be respectful and tell them you understand, and thank them for their time, leave them your card. Even if they do not give you permission, you want to be respectful, that way when they do think about it; they will be more comfortable giving you a call. If you are rude to them, they will not call you, instead they will find another group and you will ruin any chance you and your group have going in there in the future.

When you conduct your walk through, not only will

you want to take first photos, but you also will want to get some readings, EMF and some EVP work. This will help you get a base reading for your investigation later. If there are any electrical malfunctions, or high man made electrical readings you will know in advance that it may be a problem with readings in that room.

Conduct yourselves in a very professional manor, this will give you a better chance of the owner of the property giving you a recommendation to a friend, and could help build your client list.

During your investigation, you are going to want to stay in pairs, or groups of three. Never go out alone, that is for your own safety, and if you were to have an experience, you will have someone with you to verify what you saw, or heard etc.

When the investigation is a few hours away from home, you may want to consider staying in a hotel or motel for the night of the investigation, that way you do not have to drive three, four or five hours home in the middle of the night. You will have less of a chance of falling asleep behind the wheel.

When you do get home and go through your evidence, or material, you want to get it done quickly, but thoroughly. To cut back on time, you can go through your digital images at the same time as you are listening to tape recordings, or digital recordings. You may also want to consider having someone help you. If your digital images are dark, lighten them before deleting them. Sometimes they are dark and you may find that if you lighten them you may actually have something.

For Example;

This is a picture taken on an investigation to Prospect Place Mansion on September ninth two thousand six.

100 • KRISTY HINKLE AND MARIE CIPRIANO

(Photo by Kristy Hinkle. SNEP investigator)

This photograph was taken in the basement of this location, and the photo came out dark. Originally, she tossed it aside until she realized that another photo had to be lightened to completely see an image. She went back through and lightened this photo along with two hundred others and she found this apparition in the distance, which was the darkest area in the shot. It is perfectly ok to lighten photos, as long as you do not look at them only for (as seen in this picture) orbs. These are just dust orbs, the basement floor of this home is dirt and sand, this is a result of the investigators walking around stirring up dirt and dust before taking a seat in the far back of this location.

Other things to consider when analyzing your material it is a good idea to go through it more than once, just incase you may miss something.

Another thing to think of is suspect everything. Test all of the items try to find an explanation or a reason that this may have come about. Now, if you *can* reproduce it then it has to be excluded. If you are left with something unexplainable, then that is your evidence.

When you have an unexplained photo, EVP or video, this is where the other equipment comes in to help you support anything you may have picked up.

Such as EMF spikes, when you are walking around, you want to have a video camera at hand, that way you can record EMF spikes, and announce them on camera, you will have that evidence to back up your claim of paranormal activity.

If you have something to back up your claims, more than one piece of evidence from the same time and place, then it is harder for people to criticize or try to make false claims of tampering.

Many Paranormal Investigators are prepared to take many photos, even hundreds, a few from each spot, so you have a transition photo as well as your abnormal one(s).

Batteries are another important item to have, always bring spare batteries, rechargeable are good to have. At times, when paranormal activities are high, they can and will drain batteries.

If at anytime, you are unsure about the evidence you have collected, you can always take it to be analyzed by a professional, photographers, and photo developers can help with digital and 35 mm prints, videographers can help with video's and any one can help you identify an EVP. Ask a trusted friend, or a respectable Paranormal Investigator for help with these items.

If you use a 35 mm make sure to tell the processor of the film that you want back every print now matter how dark it is.

There are web sites out there that can help you if you are confused about any print or picture. You can use their photos for comparing your photos to check for a similar one that was made intentionally.

After you have ruled out any false positives, you can go back through your history report that you should have made of the location of the 'haunting' and determine weather or not you actually have something that rationalizes or confirms someone's encounter.

Tape Recorder:

A tape recorder is another very important piece of equipment. It should have a microphone sensitive enough to pick up faint sounds at a distance. It is beneficial, but not necessary, to use a machine that is voice-activated and has a tape counter. A micro cassette recorder (the kind used for taking personal notes) is ideal for ghost hunting. It is compact, yet can pick up very slight sounds. Make certain you have at least two extra blank tapes and a fresh set of batteries at all times.

Watch:

The use for a watch is obvious. It can be used to record the time into your notebook, the length of a particular phenomenon or tape recording, or just to check the time. You do not need any certain kind of watch.

Compass:

A compass will provide you with an orientation of your surroundings and lessens the chances of you getting lost. A Compass can also be used as a "spirit detector". Just as spirits may cause electrical problems with their surroundings, they also can create a lot of turmoil with magnetic sources, such as your compass. The needle may start to go crazy or refuse to work. It may also point toward a spirit, although this is not very common.

Paper and Pen:

Pen and paper are invaluable tools for any type of research, paranormal or otherwise. These can be used to sketch a map of the area you are investigating, take notes, or record data and observations. They are also useful for writing down random thoughts or feelings that you may have during an investigation.

Flour:

Yes, flour. Depending on the nature of the investigation, you may have to prevent tampering with the area you are investigating. After you have placed your equipment in the location that you want, sprinkle flour just below the area. If someone or something tampers with the equipment, chances are the flour will have been disturbed. Spirits have been known to leave impressions in the flour. If you decide to use flour as an investigative tool, make sure that you clean up the area completely when you are finished. Not cleaning up completely could reflect poorly on the paranormal investigator and could make your group look unprofessional that may follow to future cases.

Electromagnetic Detectors:

Electromagnetic Detectors detects a change in the amount of radiation in the area, it should show a noticeable difference when it encounters an abnormal energy field, such as cold spots, appliance malfunctions, etc...
All energy fields are not associated with spirit communication, but more often than not you will find increased spirit activity around places with high levels of

energy, such as power lines. Electromagnetic fields emanate from virtually everything electrical: such as computers, televisions, people (auras) and even spirits.

If your equipment has been tampered with:

Meet with your group in private; inform them of your suspicions, well away from any clients who may be in the area. The key here is discretion. If you decide that your equipment has been tampered with purposefully, calmly pack up the equipment and inform the client that the investigation has concluded. Explain to them that the equipment has been tampered with and calmly leave. Be professional and leave as promptly as possible.

Definitions:

Ghosts:

I am not too fond of this phrase, but it is what many people call a spirit.

A spirit or apparition is the energy from a life force that has been taken from the physical plane to the spirit plane, but not all of them make it to the other side. Some, who have a strong connection to something on the physical plane or have a traumatic death, can sometimes become trapped here.

Do all spirits become trapped here? No, many pass on without any problems.

Ghosts can be perceived by the living in a number of ways: through sight (apparitions), sound (voices), smell (fragrances and odors), touch - and sometimes they can just be sensed.

Haunting:

A haunting can be a number of things, lets start out with;

A Residual Haunting;

This is when there is not a real paranormal situation in a location; it is caused by a traumatic, or a highly emotional event that causes certain types of stones in the earth to copy and replay these events repeatedly, on a regular basis, nightly, weekly, and yearly or every few years. It is a normal occurrence, but is not considered a ghost, or spirit.

If a house with a residual haunting is torn down, in efforts to remove a haunting, the home built on that location will continue to have activity in the same place. For example;

If there is a residual haunting of a person walking up and down the halls in the house, the new home will have the same activity.

An Intelligent Haunting;

A true haunting that involves paranormal activity, real spirits that roam freely around a location. This is an intelligent haunting, where the spirits are in complete control of their actions, and can interact with the living.

Poltergeist:

"Poltergeist" is a German word meaning "noisy spirit." Current research indicates, however, that poltergeist activity may have nothing to do with ghosts or spirits. Since the activity seems to center around an individual, it is believed that it is caused by the subconscious mind of that individual. It is, in effect, psychokinetic activity. The individual is often under emotional, psychological or physical stress (even going through puberty). It can include such things as the physical movement of objects, lights and other electrics going on and off, channel changing on the TV's and even the manifestation of physical phenomena.

Ectoplasm, Ghostly mist;
Appearance & Characteristics:

Cloudy vaporous mist; The term was originally used to describe the substance that oozed from spirit mediums when channeling a spirit or the stuff left behind by ghosts in the all popular 'Ghost Busters' movies. It is now referred to as a mist or fog. It is usually in the colors gray, white or black but has also been seen and photographed in several other colors. Ecto has been caught on both video and all types of cameras

Orbs;
Appearance & Characteristics:

As I said on another page, I do not hold orbs to be proof of paranormal activities. Orbs are most commonly captured on a digital camera, and more often than not, end up being dust particles, bugs, moisture in the air, or raindrops.

The only time I would consider orbs as anything other than that, they need to meet certain requirements. They must give off their own light, (which can sometimes still be dust or bugs caught in more than one light source) they must have a pattern of movement, and should be visible to the naked eyes as well as the cameras.

They are the most photographed anomaly since the digital camera was inserted into the field of investigation. This is because many places you investigate do contain a lot of dust.

A HAUNTING EXISTENCE • 107

If you look closely at this photo, taken by Kristy Hinkle. You can see that there is what appears to be a face in the back. However, this image has to be discounted due to all the dust floating around in the room.

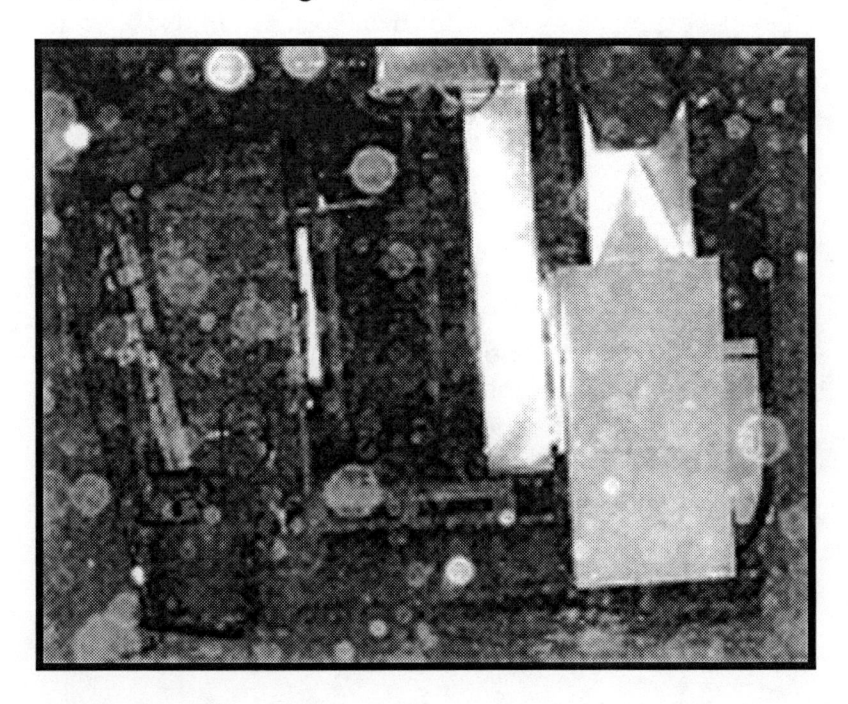

(Unsure-Discounted)

Vortex;
Appearance & Characteristics:

A vortex is believed to be a sort of tear in the lining between the spiritual realm and that of the physical plane.
This contains many spirits or entities that can come and go as they please.
This has been captured on film in sort of a funnel type shape, like tornado's or hurricanes just as a small example.
It is believed to be a hot spot for paranormal activity.

Shadow People, figures
Appearance & Characteristics:

These entities usually appear as a shadow type figure; they have a human shaped form and can be child size or the size of a full-grown man.

When they are spotted it is usually out of the corner of your eye or as they are darting through a wall, or into a near by room.

Apparitions;
Appearance & Characteristics:

Catching an apparition on film is what every Paranormal Investigator aspires to catch but seldom do. They show up in a transparent human form and wear the clothing of their period. You might also note that they normally appear faint and disfigured as in being incomplete. It should be said that an apparition can pose directly next to you and it still will not necessarily show up on film.

EMF

EMF stands for Electro Magnetic Field; it is believed that when a spirit or paranormal entity is near that it gives off a strong enough electric field that it can be picked up using an EMF detector.

EVP

Is an Electro Voice Phenomenon, a disembodied voice that appears on a recording whether you actually heard it or not.

Entities:

Entities are completely spiritual or ethereal in nature

and actually have never lived as human beings. This type of manifestation is uncommon.

Ghost:

Is Residual energy of a person, animal, or even an inanimate object. There is no life force left; a ghost simply "plays" the same scene over and over. Usually, if a person has performed a repetitious act for a long time, he or she will have left a psychic impression in that area.

Again, I cannot stress this enough.
Be safe; go in pairs of no less than two people.
Always get permission to investigate any location.
You can be arrested for trespassing.

Here are some tips for beginners
and
Frequently asked questions

Can a ghost hurt you?
'They can make contact, but hardly ever seriously hurt a human.'

Can a spirit mess with investigation equipment?
'Yes, they are known to drain batteries, turn off recorders, cameras, and video cameras

Can a spirit follow you home from an investigation?
'It is possible, but rare.'

Here are some basic things to remember when investigating:

Always get permission from the owner of the property

before you investigate. Trespassing is illegal, and dangerous.

Always treat the property and the property owners with respect.

Have a first aid kit handy, for those unexpected injuries.

Always follow group Codes of Conduct, such as smoking and alcohol consumption rules.

Arrive early enough to get settled and talk with the owners before setting up equipment.

Set up cameras in the most active places in the house or building to get the best results.

Avoid taking photos near any reflective material.

Never go out alone. Safety in numbers, always have a couple or group of two, three or four.

Always use fresh batteries and bring extras for all of your equipment and when possible a power cord to ensure battery life in computers, and such.

Be open-minded, this is the best way to ensure a great investigation and good results.

Try to stay away from dangerous locations. Do not go wandering off into isolated locations, such as a forest, woods, cornfields or cemeteries with out the proper tools, and another investigator.

Your safety is as important to your group as gathering a lot of evidence. Be safe and have fun, is the best advice any investigator can give to another one.

Be professional, if you get scared, do not scream and run, simply back up and away from what it is that has scared you. However, if you are an investigator, you should not leave the area anyways. You should try to catch the experience on film, take pictures as quickly as possible; your partner should be filming with a video camera. Take a deep breath, step back and shoot. As an investigator, it is possible that you can and will encounter the unknown. The best thing you can do is to keep calm, and do not panic. This is what you are there for; the holy grail of investigating is a full-bodied apparition. Not many investigators can say they have actually seen a full-bodied apparition, but some have! I will give you a few more photos, as examples to help you better understand your own images.

This image, taken by Kristy Hinkle, in the ballroom at Prospect Place Mansion, looks as though there could be a man standing in the corner. However, this is not actually, what you are seeing. This is a great form of Matrixing, caused by dust orbs in the air.

(False Positive)

A HAUNTING EXISTENCE • 113

This image, taken by Marie Cipriano at Fort Griswold, shows what appears to be an orb in motion. We do not get excited about orbs, but at the time this photo was taken, the woman in the shot was talking about a high EMF spike, of nearly 7.2 on the meter. That is the only verification of this image that we have other than at the time this was taken and the spike was reported, there was a video camera turned on the women in this photo.

This photo was also taken by Marie Cipriano on the same investigation.

There was no one in our group sitting on this rock; we have no explanation for why there appears to be a person sitting here on this rock.

A HAUNTING EXISTENCE • 115

This photo was taken in the home of Kristy Hinkle many years ago. Here you can see how easily a reflection of light can be manipulated to appear paranormal; when in actuality it is nothing more than tricks of light. The flash from the 35mm camera reflected off the metal on the window frame and created this elaborate show of light streaks.

(False Positive

This is for all those who wish to get to know me better.

You have read about some of my experiences and now I wish to share with you some private thoughts, and moments in my life. The main reason I am the way I am.

My name is Kristy Hinkle,
And this is the story behind the woman.

A HAUNTING EXISTENCE;
THE STORY BEHIND THIS WOMAN.

More than you will ever need to know about me.
For as long as I can remember, I have been persecuted for my beliefs and for what I see. I cannot remember a time when I was taken seriously.

Something as simple as a sighting from the spiritual realm, or something as massive as the fact that two missing girls were not run a ways. No one wants to believe that there are such things in this world that cannot be explained; I on the other hand, have been trying my best to change the opinions of those people whose lives touch mine.

I try to be sensitive about their feelings of things, the way they see the world and spirituality. I do not tell them they are wrong, just that their views are different from mine as well as other peoples. I do not try to change who they are, just the way they view me and those like me.

I have been called a psychic, based on what I have seen, and relayed to people, I do not credit my self with such a title. If I am a psychic, I say myself with all honesty that I am not a very good one!

I am not someone you will find at the state fair laying out tarot cards, and telling you of the destiny that a waits with your future love, or life long down fall.

My abilities are more simple, and easier to understand. I have tried the tarot thing, I am not very good at it, I have tried gazing at a crystal ball to no avail, I have even tried reading tea leaves, people, and (goddess forgive me) a Ouija board.

None of which were very effective, for me at least. However, they may work for others. I used to be good at, what I have always called Prophetic Dreaming, and I am very good at saying things out of context and having them happen within days, sometime hours.

I cannot really explain what it is exactly, I am not a trance medium, and I do not talk very openly with the spirit world. To be quite frank it sort of scares me!

I am not going to give you all sorts of technical terms about this; I will have to make you understand exactly what it is I am talking about. What I have done in the past, before I knew what it was, and now that I do know but still, sometimes, do not pay attention to it.

I am going to take you back many years ago. Forgive my fuzzy memory; it has been a long time.

Some examples would be that one-day sitting in our living room having a normal conversation with Jessey and our friend Andy, about some of the natural disasters, going on in the world such as hurricanes, typhoons and such, out of the blue I blurted out that there was going to be a horrible earthquake. Andy assumed I was talking about California and threw it out there, that people had been saying that for years and he had not seen it yet. I looked at him, and said I have never said that and I am not saying it now. I think it will be in an Asian region, and there will be thousands of lives lost.

Nearly two weeks later, it happened. On my way into work early one morning, they broke in with some news that South East Asia, along with a few other countries had been hit with a massive earthquake, It hit in the middle of the night, no one knew it was coming, tens of thousands were dead.

I had relayed this to a few people at the place where I had worked at the time, and when they heard the news on the radio as well, they were stunned. I had many questions to answer when I got to work that day.

This is interesting; some say you are not psychic about yourself. Are you a freak if you are?

I have been known to predict things for not only close family and friends, but also myself. Such as being fired from a job, I packed up my stuff a few days before for no reason that I had really known, I had also told a co-worker I would not see her the following Monday, and by the end of the week, I was let go.

I have seen and talked to the spirit guides of other people as well as my own.

I told one girl that I did not even know, that I had met on-line about a party she was having when she never told me about it, also about her stuffed animal collection on her bed.

That was sort of like a verification test the girl had questioned something I had said on an internet forum and I answered her questions with amazing accuracy.

I have been known to warn people about getting pulled over by the police, and get that validated when they actually do a day or two later. They still do not listen to me, but I am getting used to that.

I did not used make a habit of telling people what I was seeing, not for a while at least; when it did not subside within a few years, I was starting to get worried. I had to learn how to control it, and did so with the help of books and informational CD's, released by world-renowned psychics.

By using it and not hiding it, it became easier for me to tap into it when I wanted to and not so much blurt out things that I should not have at the wrong times.

My abilities are a gift, I cherish them every day, and I use them to help as much as I can.

Unfortunately, I am not that great at talking to the deceased. There are some family members and friends of mine that I would love to talk to again, but I have yet to hear from any of them.

I do appreciate the little signs they throw my way, but I would like to have a real conversation with them.

ne sign that I could not ignore, when I knew something was happening, was when I was Sixteen years old, I had been taking an after school nap on the sofa in the living room, I believe at the time there were a few of my siblings in there. I apparently sat up and started talking in my sleep; they said that I told them that two of our friends who went missing only a few days earlier had not run away as everyone thought. They asked me how I knew and I said, I did not know. Then I lay back down and continued my nap.

That made me start thinking; I went searching for answers when the bodies of our friends had turned up murdered a few days after that.

Many of my dreams had come true before, but they were not about anything I really thought hard about, like something would happen at school, who one of my friends would be dating and when, and even about an old friends return from another state where he had lived for a few years.

Do you ever get a 'feeling' as if something is wrong? Well, for me when I get that feeling I am usually right. This happened in Nineteen Ninety-Six. My then boyfriend and I were sitting on a friends back porch talking when at nearly ten in the evening we both stopped and looked at each other, he asked me if I could feel that, and I said yes. Something was different the winds had changed. There was a horrible feeling in the air. Something bad was coming, but neither of us really knew what.

Later that night, I had stayed at my friend's house we got the call. A friend of ours had died in a car accident. This goes with the story, A Visit From A Friend, this is what happened before the visit. We were in shock as we pulled into the driveway at my house, we found my then boyfriend and his friend standing there waiting for us.

He and his friend had gone looking for Jared when he did not arrive home by curfew, and his mom called. They had found the mangled car, and had been detained by the police so they could not go and tell any of the family or friends before the police on the scene could notify his parents.

Fast-forward to only a few years ago, maybe two years by now. I was on my way home from the place I worked at the time, when a co-worker drove past me going fast. My minds eye suddenly went black and I saw his car flipping on a road somewhere. I freaked out about this, and told Jessey about it, he reassured me that I was over reacting to this. He said that I saw the guy flying by me on the road and that is what I pictured happening because of the way he drives.

This did calm me down, until the following Monday when our boss told us all that it had in fact happen and he was in an accident where he had been drinking and flipped his car on the highway.

I immediately turned to another co-worker and told her everything about that past Friday night. She just looked at me in shock; I still cannot believe that I did not call him and check on him that day or tell him what I saw.

I was still trying to come to grips with what I was seeing, as it was becoming more frequent and becoming reality more and more often. I did not know if there was something wrong with me, you know like that movie where the guy has a brain tumor and it made him telekinetic.

It was not until I saw Sylvia Browne for the first time on the Montel show that I started wondering about my self. I looked more into it, and read some books, that is when I knew what it had to be.

Trying to suppress it did not work, so maybe, if I attempted to work on it, and refine it I could help people. Even to this day though, people have a hard time believing what I tell them. Even those who have seen the reality of it many times before.

Do you know what it is like to be the black sheep in your family? Be the strange one?

I do.

I make different choices, and I know things I should not know. I have gone through this for a long time. My mother knows that it is not something I am making up, but I still have other family members who believe that it is, to quote one person "It is just a phase, that I need to grow out of already." I love that statement, because if it were a phase, why have I not grown out of it by now, I am Twenty-Seven years old. It has been many years since this started, that is a long phase.

I have found salvation through my religion, and people who can help me deal with this. I am a Proud Pagan, and I have many friends in the Pagan/Wiccan community. They have never accused me of going through a phase over the last eleven years. I am lucky to have them in my life. I can talk to them about anything that I need to get off my chest, and anything that is going on in my life.

I cannot go into much detail about my visions, and I am not going to put in here any thoughts I have on the future. I will tell you, As a Paranormal Investigator, these abilities come in handy at times, but I do not use them to investigate. Like many other groups, Southern New England Paranormal takes a scientific approach to our investigating, there are no psychic readings, and we do not hold séances, or use other psychic tools to track down spirits. Unlike many, I refuse to open up that much for anything from the other side.

This ability does not always work either. You know sort of like a light bulb. One day it works, and the next it blows out. That is the way I feel about it sometimes. I know what most people in the paranormal field think about 'psychics' but like I previously stated. I do not consider myself a 'psychic'. I look at it more like, getting snippets of information that I should not be getting. Sometimes I wonder why me, but other times I am glad it did happen to me. I wish I could explain it better. But what I can tell you is sometimes when I get this information, it is more like, my mind goes blank and I can 'see' in my head what is going to happen. Sometimes it is just like a fleeting thought, something I know or have known. Then other times, I can hear it in my head, like someone telling me about something. Yes, I hear voices. No, I am not mental, though I can introduce you to people who would beg to differ with that thought.

On a more personal note.

This is not a subject, which I am comfortable talking about. Because of all of the skeptics who have made it near impossible for anyone with abilities to come forward. I have been yelled at, teased, I have been the butt of an entire work places jokes, I have been given horrible nick names by these awful people, and at times my own property has been damaged. I have received nasty e-mails because of this, I have been called Evil, and a devil worshiper, (how can you worship something you do not believe in?) and I have people who have accused me of child abuse for teaching my beliefs to my children. I have even been accused of hexing people, making their lives hard on them or giving them money troubles. Anything that went wrong in certain people's lives was always my fault I had cursed them. Now do you really believe in that? I hope this person reads this and finally realizes how stupid she really was.

The Wiccan/Pagan community has taken many blows

from churches and other religious organizations trying to keep us from having our celebrations. In a country that is supposed to have the right to choose our religion and not be persecuted for our beliefs why, are we always the first to be attacked?

Why on earth would people accuse us of harming children, or animals, or any life for that matter? We hold all these things sacred. We are not child molesters, or murderers.

The only thing I hope to achieve from this rant is a little peace. Try to get the word out, that people are different, but no matter what our religion, color, talents, gifts or abilities, we are still human. Do not accuse us of things when you are the one who is too ignorant to do the research before you make these accusations. Those who live in glass houses should not through stones…

I am finished with that, it was just something I had to get out of my system; I am tired of being the butt of people's jokes, and just another person for them to put down. My children will grow up knowing the traditions of both the Pagan religion, and the Christian religion, and I do not care who does not like this idea.

Want some more information on me?

We are now at the present, in the year Two-Thousand Six. I am now a stay at home mother, working with Southern New England Paranormal Co-founder Marie Cipriano on this book, I am a member of Southern Ohio Paranormal Research, an Honorary member of Springfield Ghost Hunters Society, and a former member of the affiliate group, Southern New England Paranormal.

I have two wonderful children and a great family. Most have been very supportive of my many ventures, and with my search to find what my purpose on this planet is.

In recent months, I have become friends with some of the most famous of all Ghost Hunters, The Atlantic Paranormal Society, (also known as TAPS). Grant Wilson is one of the greatest people to talk with. He is very intelligent and informative. He did not mind answering all of my stupid questions.

They are a great group of people and I am honored to know them, and I would love to go on an investigation with them.

With all my many ventures in recent months, I do not really have much spare time. I am constantly working on this book and a possible second one, taking care of my house and kids, working with Paranormal Investigators, traveling to and from Akron Ohio for different reasons, and have been traveling to and from Connecticut. I will not have any spare time to be with my friends. I do try as hard as I can to keep in touch with them, through the phone or through e-mails.

I find that even if you cannot spend a whole lot of time with friends and family, that the quality of time you spend with them is in fact more important than the amount of time you spend there. I know we all wish we could spend everyday with our family and friends, but some of us are just really busy, even people like me who do not work out side of the home, other than on weekend ventures on investigations, but remain very busy regardless.

I absolutely love being a Paranormal Investigator. A friend of mine once told me if I was interested in it, then I should not care what people think of it and just do it. I love that person. They know who they are.

I typically like everyone unless they give me a reason not to. However, I never need them to give me a reason; I seem to know when someone is bad news. As if, I have a sixth sense about people. Sometimes I can tell from talking to them one time, looking at them (which is rare, but it happens) or even just talking to them on the phone.

If they are bad news, I typically stay away from them, and watch as they dig their own holes.

Part of this was supposed to be in a book all its own, then I realized, no one wants to read all of that about someone they do not even know. That is when I decided to contact Marie and see if she would be interested in working with me to write this.

After teaming up with Marie, we decided to write it this way, to give people a sense that there are other's out there who have had many experiences like theirs, in here are mostly mine, but I know there are people out there who will not talk about this with just anyone. I want to help people understand that they are not alone. Others who did not believe in such things are affected by this every day. Take the Marion Investigation for example. The male homeowner never believed in paranormal activity, until he came face to face with it. Even then, he was reluctant to ask me for help.

I know this is more information than anyone would ever want to know about me, but there are some who have asked for this information so I decided to include this section for their benefit. As many people who really know me would tell you. I am not a shy person; I like to be open and honest with anyone. If they have the guts to ask such personal questions, I think they should be rewarded with an honest answer. I always give an honest answer. However, not all people appreciate how honest I am about such personal things, but that is their problem.

Kristy Hinkle

Final Note; Since the completion of this book, I have left Southern New England Paranormal and have joined a more local group that I have worked with before, which is reflected in my biography, Southern Ohio Paranormal Research.

I do still keep in contact with the founder of Southern New England Paranormal and co-writer of this book, Marie Cipriano.

I also will continue working with them if my services are requested upon any of my trips to the New England area.

Southern Ohio Paranormal Research, and Southern New England Paranormal are affiliate groups and will work together on co-op investigations in the future.

I wish to share with you some things about me, and moments in my life. The explanation behind this woman.

My name is Marie Cipriano,

A HAUNTING EXISTENCE; PART 2
THE STORY BEHIND THIS WOMAN.

My name is Marie. I am the Founder of Southern New England Paranormal. I have a beautiful daughter named Anya. She is the love of my life and also the most precious thing in the world to me. I had a lot of complications after I had her and I almost died two days after she was born. The hospital that my daughter was born in was to blame. I had an emergency C-section and with that come an Epidural (The spinal pain medication where you are numb from the waist down). The Hospital was neglectful to watch and monitor the fluids being released from my body. There was no fluids being released from my body and in return I was diagnosed with Congestive Heart Failure. I spent three days in the
 Intensive Care Unit. Yes, that means my heart was shutting down. I had X-rays done and they showed that I had fluid around my heart that was literally squeezing the life out of me. Next step for the doctors was to remove the fluid away from my heart. They removed three liters of fluid from around my heart. Yes three Liters. (That is two

and a half large bottles of soda). I had to undergo extensive testing to make sure that was indeed the only problem that I was facing. I underwent Radioactive testing, Dye Therapy testing, more x-rays, Full body scans, Stress Tests. While I was having all these tests done, the worst part for me was trying to be strong minded and optimistic about staying alive to see my two-day-old newborn daughter. I was also thinking "Please God do not let my daughter grow up without her mother", " Please let me be ok so I can receive the love from the life that I just had".

I am a Licensed Security Guard through the State of CT. I work for Securitas Security. Securitas is a world leader in security. Securitas Group has operations in more than 30 countries, primarily in Europe and North America. We are a world leader in security, with annual sales of approximately $6 billion. Every day, more than 200,000 employees work to carry out our mission of protecting homes, work places and community. With a sharp focus on security, we provide security services in close cooperation with customers. To this end, business areas have been added and the service content has been specialized and developed. Our business areas are Guard Services, Alarm Systems and Cash

Handling. Securitas Group entered the U.S. market in 1999 with the acquisition of the security company, Pinkteron's, Inc. By 2001, Securitas Group had successfully acquired seven more U.S. guarding companies, including Burns International. In July 2003, the combined American acquisitions became Securitas Security Services USA, Inc., a leading security company that works with more than 80 percent of the Fortune 1000 companies and has annual revenues in excess of $2.5 billion. Securitas Group is a market leader and has been listed on the Swedish Stock Exchange since 1991.Securitas is the most locally focused security company in the United States. Every day, more than 100,000 security officers at more than 600 branch offices throughout the country provide unmatched security solutions to meet the specific needs of thousands of businesses. Internationally, the Securitas Group has 2,000 branch offices located in 30 countries. Securitas USA's services include patrols and inspections, access control, reception and badging services, security console operators, alarm response, and specialized client requested services. I am certified in CPR, and First Aid. I am looking into going back to school to get my Private Investigators License, and also to get my Bail Bonds License.

I am a Spiritualist. We believe in Infinite Intelligence, and believe that the existence and personal identity of the individual continue after the change called death. We, in Modern Spiritualism, know that all flows according to Natural Law. Where the ancients believed in the supernatural, miracles and magic, punishment and rewards, we believe in the natural, God's Laws, growth and love. We are a truth seeking religion that incorporates science and testing as a part of our philosophy. Often the people of the past thought of phenomena as the work of devils and demons. Some religions today still see communication in this manner. We know that the phenomenon is a work through those in the Spirit World and that we attract to us spirit guides that correspond to the level of our vibration.

Spiritualists come from every walk of life. We are bankers, builders, nurses, teachers, bookkeepers, and sales clerks, electricians - any and all professions are attracted to Spiritualism. Every place you find thinking men and women coming together, you will find Spiritualists. Spiritualism is a science, philosophy and religion that satisfy your logic, your mind and your heart. As the population contemplates the current conditions in the world today, they are seeking a greater understanding of the purpose of life and what can be done to improve individual life situations and the circumstances of the world.

Spiritualism gives a person the key that can be used to find the answers she/he seeks. Spiritualism provides the knowledge that by using prayer and meditation, we can become more aware of our responsibilities to ourselves and to others.

Through this inner awareness and guidance received through spirit communications, a person takes the necessary actions to improve his or her own life and contributes to the improved welfare of the entire human race. Spiritualism is the KEY that sets humanity free! Free to live and grow in the physical through love and law, and free because we know that life is continuous, the spirit never dies. "There is no death, there are no dead."

I have been interested in the Paranormal all my life. I have had a few

Experiences of this kind and also some in the area of crypto zoology. Being in the paranormal field is in my blood (I can't live without it). I am truly blessed to be best friends with and working with one of the greatest woman I know (Kristy Hinkle). Many people just naturally have a curiosity about the supernatural and the unexplained; they intuitively know that current scientific models don't have all the answers.

Although many consider the paranormal nonsense, unscientific or at the least a harmless diversion, it could represent something far deeper.

What we commonly refer to as "paranormal phenomena" - whatever that is - could be a glimpse into the very subconscious of human beings and how our minds might interact with the universe around us. Such experiences are called paranormal because they are, using the dictionary definition of the word, "scientifically unexplainable." The word means beyond (from the Greek, Para) normal. It includes experiences, events and phenomena that, as Fox Mulder used to say on 'The X-Files,' cannot be catalogued, categorized or easily referenced. Weird things, which do not fit our everyday view of the world. Such experiences remain scientifically unexplainable because they are difficult, if not impossible, to examine by the scientific method.

They are spontaneous, fleeting moments and largely unrepeatable.

There is usually no tangible proof of them having occurred; stuff that cannot usually be brought into a lab to be probed, dissected, photographed or tested. So they are most often dismissed as figments of the imagination, hallucinations or psychological phenomena. And, of course, many such experiences could be just that. As relatively rare as paranormal phenomena are, however, they are not uncommon either.

There are hundreds of thousands of first-hand accounts like those listed above (and some far stranger) to be found in the literature, and now on the Web.

None of them are explainable from scientific reference points, yet they have been a part of the human experience since the beginning of recorded history. In fact, a person is far more likely to have a paranormal experience than he or she is to win the lottery or be struck by lightning. You may have had one yourself. Ask your friends and relatives. Everyone has a story of some unexplained event. They might not all be valid; maybe most of them aren't. But all we need is one valid, inexplicable event to say that perhaps the world doesn't quite work exactly the way the science books say it does all the time. Of course there are more than one event; there are many.

A New Understanding

It's this abundance of anecdotal evidence that should lead us to conclude that there is much more to life on this planet than we are currently aware of or understand.

Because science cannot yet explain these phenomena

does not mean they do not exist or are not true. And it does not mean that science will not someday understand these phenomena.

In fact, we may be on the verge of understanding a lot of these weird goings-on:

Research being conducted at the respected universities around the world has demonstrated the effect of psychokinesis - the ability of the mind alone to significantly affect a random outcome.

The rigorous scientific experiments of Dr. Gary E. Schwartz are proving that human consciousness survives after death.

The study of quantum mechanics, where subatomic matter is seen to behave in a most unusual and illogical way (and might be connected to human consciousness), could in the coming decades lead to a scientific understanding of much of what we now consider paranormal phenomena.

If you have any questions I can be contacted at: fairuzact@southernnewenglandparanormal.com

Thank You
Marie Cipriano

A HAUNTING EXISTENCE • 139

Marie Cipriano